D0090618

Praise for
The Life-Giving Leader

"Tyler is a good friend of mine. He doesn't just think like a leader; he lives like one. He dropped everything to drive an hour and be at my side, simply because he knew I needed a friend. When he arrived, he didn't tell me what to do but instead reminded me of who I am. This is what great leaders do—it's what this book is about, and it's written by a guy who services what he sells."

> —Bob Goff, *New York Times* best-selling author of *Love Does* and *Everybody, Always*

"This book will absolutely set your soul on fire to become the most authentic, determined, and impactful leader you can be. If you need a fresh wind or are simply looking for a dynamic leadership resource, you should read *The Life-Giving Leader*."

> —Lysa TerKeurst, *New York Times* best-selling author and president of Proverbs 31 Ministries

"Fresh. Important. Helpful. Whether you're guiding one person or a massive organization, leadership can be a heavy load. When we try to take the responsibility of carrying all that weight ourselves, we'll eventually be crushed under it or burned out by it. In *The Life-Giving Leader,* Tyler Reagin affirms God's design for leaders by removing undue burdens and pointing you to the essentials that will multiply your impact. You'll be relieved to know that this resource won't give you another checklist to accomplish. Rather, it will give you a deep breath of the fresh air from God's Word. It will shift your focus back to His sufficiency to carry out the good work that He began in you. As you consider resources to help you become a better and more whole leader, I hope you'll add this one to your short list."

> —Louie Giglio, pastor of Passion City Church and founder of Passion Conferences

"In my many years of interacting with leaders, I have yet to see a person who understands the dynamics of leadership better than Tyler Reagin. He exemplifies the love of Jesus perfectly. His wisdom and useful applications will allow readers to shatter outdated paradigms and rebuild their philosophy about leadership. Readers *must* make time to absorb Tyler's knowledge and immediately apply it to their lives."

—BUZZ WILLIAMS, Virginia Tech basketball coach

"The Life-Giving Leader is more than a book; it's a powerful blueprint that shows us how to truly lead as God calls us to—so that we can positively influence others and the world. Trust me, this is not just another leadership book. Tyler shows us how to lead with true power so we can energize, encourage, inspire, and give life to others. I guarantee it will be one of the most powerful leadership books you'll read this year."

—JON GORDON, best-selling author of *The Power of Positive Leadership*

"The Life-Giving Leader is the book we have all been waiting for! Tyler offers inspiring, thought-provoking, and powerful lessons in unlocking the truest and best version of yourself! This is a must-read."

—DEVON FRANKLIN, producer and *New York Times* best-selling author

"Tyler, a passionate lover of Jesus, has focused his life on nurturing the potential within others. He is also an extraordinary example of servant leadership, possessing personal understanding of the cost and value of the leadership journey. *The Life-Giving Leader* is a thought-provoking rendering of Tyler's unique insights into what it means to be a life-giving leader who lives for a purpose far beyond self. To quote Tyler: 'The pursuit of life-giving leadership begins and ends with Jesus.'"

—BRIAN HOUSTON, global senior pastor of Hillsong Church and author of *There Is More*

"I can't think of a better person to write on life-giving leadership than Tyler Reagin. His approach to leading the people around us is not only refreshing, but it is also Jesus's model. And when we lead *with* God, instead of *for* God, we can step back and let Him go crazy through us."

—Jennie Allen, author of *Nothing to Prove,* and founder
and visionary of the IF:Gathering

"There are two kinds of people in this world. There are those who walk into a room and say, 'Here I am!' And there are those who walk into a room and say, 'There you are!' In this important and timely book, my friend Tyler will teach you how to become the kind of leader who notices and enhances the lives of those around you. You'll see how new levels of usefulness in your own life are unlocked in the process. The upside-down secret that will change everything is that *giving,* not keeping, is the key to receiving."

—Levi Lusko, author of *I Declare War: Four Keys
to Winning the War with Yourself*

"We are all called to step into our God-given destiny, but we often get distracted trying to lead like everyone else—rather than being the leader God uniquely designed us to be. In *The Life-Giving Leader,* Tyler shares practical leadership principles that will equip you to stay laser focused on the plan God has for your life as a leader."

—Christine Caine, best-selling author and founder of A21
and Propel Women

"When Tyler told me he was writing a book on leadership, I instantly thought, *Yup—makes perfect sense.* Tyler's life-giving leadership is real, tested, and replicable because he's truly a builder. He builds people who build the church that Jesus is building. Tyler is the real deal—no one talks it, walks it, and lives it like he does."

—Judah Smith, lead pastor of Churchome and *New York Times*
best-selling author of *Jesus Is _____.*

THE
LIFE
GIVING
LEADER

Forewords by Craig Groeschel and Andy Stanley

THE
LIFE
GIVING
LEADER

LEARNING TO LEAD FROM
YOUR TRUEST SELF

TYLER REAGIN
PRESIDENT OF CATALYST

WATERBROOK

THE LIFE-GIVING LEADER

Details in some anecdotes and stories have been changed to protect the identities of the persons involved.

Hardcover ISBN 978-0-7352-9094-5
eBook ISBN 978-0-7352-9095-2

Copyright © 2018 by Excolo Coaching & Consulting

Cover design by Corinne Kutz; cover photograph by Matt Cherubino

Published in association with Yates & Yates, www.yates2.com.

Published in the United States by WaterBrook, an imprint of the Crown Publishing Group, a division of Penguin Random House LLC, New York.

Library of Congress Cataloging-in-Publication Data
Names: Reagin, Tyler, author.
Title: The life-giving leader : learning to lead from your truest self / Tyler Reagin.
Description: First Edition. | Colorado Springs : WaterBrook, 2018.
Identifiers: LCCN 2018000552| ISBN 9780735290945 (hardcover) | ISBN 9780735290952 (electronic)
Subjects: LCSH: Leadership—Religious aspects—Christianity.
Classification: LCC BV4597.53.L43 R43 2018 | DDC 253—dc23
LC record available at https://lccn.loc.gov/2018000552

Printed in the United States of America
2018—First Edition

10 9 8 7 6 5 4 3 2 1

SPECIAL SALES
Most WaterBrook books are available at special quantity discounts when purchased in bulk by corporations, organizations, and special-interest groups. Custom imprinting or excerpting can also be done to fit special needs. For information, please email specialmarketscms@penguinrandom house.com or call 1-800-603-7051.

Carrie: Not only do I dedicate this book to you, but I also know I owe much of who I am to you. Thank you for living this crazy journey by my side!

Nate and Charlie: This is the culmination of God's leadership in my life; therefore, this book is dedicated to you two so that you will always know what your dad believes about leadership and faith.

Contents

Foreword by Craig Groeschel

Years ago when I first met Tyler Reagin, two things stood out immediately. First, Tyler is crazy passionate about Jesus. Second, Tyler is obsessed with building great leaders. During our first conversation, I knew instantly we would become friends. But I had no idea we'd end up working closely together to empower leaders who love the local church.

Now, almost a decade later, I've had the privilege of serving with and learning from one of the greatest servant leaders I've ever met. In title, Tyler is president of Catalyst. But his heart and gifts extend far beyond any title or label. Tyler's love for people is contagious. I've watched him inspire thousands of people from onstage and in the next moment focus on encouraging an insecure intern. I've seen Tyler strategically solve complex problems and intentionally shape a culture over time. I've watched him win the trust of spiritually disinterested people and lead them closer to the things of God.

Because of Tyler's leadership and vision, he's gathered some of the nation's top leaders to generously invest in others at Catalyst conferences in cities around the world.

One of my mentors told me you can learn from any leader. Sometimes you learn what you *want* to do. Other times you learn what you *never* want to do. Unfortunately, most of us have been exposed to leaders we don't want to emulate.

If you have ever served under a controlling, critical, or insecure leader, you know firsthand the challenges dysfunctional leadership can create. You might have felt hesitant, afraid, demoralized, or discouraged. Unhealthy leaders create unhealthy environments. They can suck the life out of an organization.

Thankfully, Tyler shows us a better way to lead in his new book, *The Life-Giving Leader*. Rather than demanding loyalty, a life-giving leader first extends trust. Instead of controlling followers, a life-giving leader empowers other leaders. Rather than talking down to people, a life-giving leader develops people so they can do more than they thought possible.

If you want to grow in your leadership, this is the perfect book for you. But let me warn you: there are no shortcuts. The road isn't easy. As I've heard Tyler say before, "Leadership isn't easy. It's difficult because it matters. It changes people. It's valuable. And things of value require sacrifice."

I promise you, the principles Tyler writes about are practical, powerful, and time tested. This book will push you, stretch you, and help you grow. And as you apply what you learn, you will become more like the One who gave His life that we might live.

You will become a life-giving leader.

—Craig Groeschel, senior pastor of Life.Church

Foreword by Andy Stanley

Great leaders breathe life into the leaders around them.

Insecure leaders, not so much.

You will do one or the other. There is no third option.

You *will* be included in the stories of the men and women who reported to you or worked alongside you. When they tell their stories, you'll get a mention. Either you'll be the boss, manager, or team lead who spoke to their potential, allowed them to shine, and was quick to give credit where it was due.

Or you'll be that other boss.

The one who hoarded the credit. The one so consumed by his own career that he gave little or no thought to helping the next generation. The one easily threatened by new talent, fresh ideas, and outside-the-box thinking.

Regardless of your personal success and achievements, when the folks who reported to you tell their stories, you'll be scored "pass" or "fail." While it's unlikely they'll use this exact terminology, they will remember you as either a life-giving leader or a leader who drained the life out of them. You'll be celebrated as the leader who put wind in their sails. Or you'll be remembered as a headwind—someone who impeded the progress and achievements of those you led.

The choice is yours.

The choice is yours every day.

As counterintuitive as it may sound, it is actually in your best interests to become, as my friend Tyler puts it, a life-giving leader. The value of a life is always determined by how much of it is given away. Funerals teach us that. Over the course of your marketplace or ministry career, you'll have endless opportunities to give your life away. What you do with those opportunities will define you. How you respond to those opportunities will determine your legacy. Live for yourself and you'll have only yourself to show for yourself in the end. But when you give your life away—when you choose to breathe life into the people around you—you'll not only add value to the lives of others, but you'll make your life more valuable as well. Tyler summarizes it perfectly:

When life flows, influence grows.

I've known, worked with, and worked for Tyler for over twelve years. He is the embodiment of this book. His personal and career successes underscore the enduring principles he teases out for his readers. If you want to have more than yourself to show for yourself, this book will help get you there.

—Andy Stanley, North Point Ministries

THE
LIFE
GIVING
LEADER

A Charge

Have you ever felt as if God has given you a message to share? How about a theme your life has been focused on? If you had one chance to tell the world the thoughts that guide you, what would you say?

These interrelated questions pushed me to write this book. Among examples of poor leadership and glimmers of hope in great leadership, I feel called to steward one message. It all comes down to *life-giving leadership.*

Life-giving leadership can change the game. It can change work environments almost instantly. It can change church culture. It should be the norm.

Early in this journey, I asked my sons what they thought I should write about. I was curious to see where they think my passions lie.

My older son responded with a smirk, quickly saying, "Leadership." He laughed and said that's all I talk about anyway. My younger son followed up with a one-word answer: "Jesus." I told them if I wrote a book on Jesus and leadership, then I could probably cover most of my thoughts on the life I want to lead.

The pursuit of life-giving leadership begins and ends with Jesus. My faith is central to my leadership, and it has directed my life for twenty-five years and will continue to do so. But why am I writing about leadership and not some other pressing need?

First, we're seeing a crisis of leadership that won't be addressed until Jesus followers step up and through their leadership bring life to others. Whether you serve as a leader on the staff of a church, work in education, lead a nonprofit organization, or head a for-profit corporation, it is essential that you see the importance of how you lead. The way you lead is mission-critical for great organizations, because as a leader, you represent something bigger than just yourself.

Jesus gives us the best picture of how leaders should lead: leadership should focus on bringing life to others. Jesus brought life to people during His time on earth, and He continues to do so today. It only makes sense that leading and life-giving go hand in hand.

Leaders, what if your greatest legacy was that people found life through your leadership? Imagine if your fingerprint was seen not only in your organization, team, and family but also in *many* organizations, teams, and families?

WELCOME TO LIFE-GIVING LEADERSHIP

One of my favorite passages in the Old Testament book of Ezekiel is known as the valley of dry bones. Have you ever felt as if your soul and even life itself had become brittle and dry, lacking fullness and abundance? I believe we all have at one time or another. That's why I'd like you to read this passage with leadership in mind. Think about work environments that felt similar to this awful valley.

> The hand of the LORD was on me, and he brought me out by the
> Spirit of the LORD and set me in the middle of a valley; it was full
> of bones. He led me back and forth among them, and I saw a great

many bones on the floor of the valley, bones that were very dry. He asked me, "Son of man, can these bones live?"

I said, "Sovereign LORD, you alone know."

Then he said to me, "Prophesy to these bones and say to them, 'Dry bones, hear the word of the LORD! This is what the Sovereign LORD says to these bones: *I will make breath enter you, and you will come to life.* I will attach tendons to you and make flesh come upon you and cover you with skin; *I will put breath in you, and you will come to life.* Then you will know that I am the LORD.'" (37:1–6, NIV)

Have you ever been in a situation where someone spoke life into you and it was as though breath entered your lungs? Have you gone through seasons that were so long and dry that when something life-giving came around it was like breathing in new life? That is the type of impact life-giving leaders can have on the people around them. With the Lord's help, we can breathe life into those we've been entrusted to lead.

The passage in Ezekiel continues:

I prophesied as I was commanded. And as I was prophesying, there was a noise, a rattling sound, and the bones came together, bone to bone. I looked, and tendons and flesh appeared on them and skin covered them, but there was no breath in them.

Then he said to me, "Prophesy to the breath; prophesy, son of man, and say to it, 'This is what the Sovereign LORD says: Come, breath, from the four winds and breathe into these slain, that they may live.'" So I prophesied as he commanded me, and breath entered them; they came to life and stood up on their feet—a vast army.

Then he said to me: "Son of man, these bones are the people of Israel. They say, 'Our bones are dried up and our hope is gone;

we are cut off.' Therefore prophesy and say to them: 'This is what
the Sovereign LORD says: My people, I am going to open your
graves and bring you up from them; I will bring you back to the
land of Israel. Then you, my people, will know that I am the LORD,
when I open your graves and bring you up from them. I will put
my Spirit in you and you will live, and I will settle you in your own
land. Then you will know that I the LORD have spoken, and I have
done it, declares the LORD.'" (verses 7–14, NIV)

This prophecy of hope was given to people who were losing hope. They
were as dry as bones and that's when God breathed life. We know that God
could have given life to Israel completely on His own, with no one else on
hand to assist. But instead, He chose to partner with Ezekiel, asking the
prophet to breathe life into the dry bones. God has always chosen to love
people through His people. He uses His children. He uses His leaders.

In this book, I plan to show you that you have been called to be a life-
giving leader. Just as the Lord restored hope and life to Israel, He can also
partner with you to restore hope and life to those around you. Your spiritual act of worship could be to lead well.

As you partner with God to become a life-giving leader, you must
learn to lead from your truest self. You can give life to others only when it's
flowing from a place of authentic leadership. That requires you to be you.
If you try to lead using the approach taken by someone else, the flow of life
that comes from you will be blocked.

Think of a leader whose leadership had the effect of taking life from
you. I don't mean your physical life but your inner vitality. I'm referring to
the type of leader who drained your time, energy, and spiritual well-being.
I don't know anyone who would want to partner with such a leader.

Now let's take this exercise a step further. Is it possible you could be
leading in a similar way?

I invite you to join me on a journey I've been on for more than two decades. We can learn together what life-giving leadership looks like (and what it doesn't look like). And I can assure you that you will never regret exploring this path to leading as Jesus did, the way of the life-giving leader.

Let's lead as if people's lives depend on our leadership, because they do. Let's pour life into others to build a life-giving legacy of leadership. There is no greater pursuit for our leadership than to seek first the kingdom and to lead from that posture. God will serve alongside you, and it will be the most fulfilling adventure of your life. People are worth your best.

1

It's Just Your Personality

You Are Uniquely Created to Lead

f you are not successful, it's probably just your personality." I've actually been told this twice in my life. Once by a leader and another time by a friend—people I trusted. Even though the words pierced my heart, they later turned out to be a gift. But in those moments I was really hurt.

The second time was definitely painful, but it was also profound. I now know that the most important leadership moment for me was also my most difficult. It felt like failure, but God used it to change my leadership and me forever. And I hope, because of that pivotal moment, He has changed many other leaders through my leadership.

I wonder if the people who said these words even remember the situation. I still believe they were trying to be helpful, and the message they delivered *was* helpful. Just not in the way they intended.

I had two thoughts when I heard the words.

First, I thought about a couple of people who were wired as I was and who had been very successful.

Second, and this was the game changer—if what was said about me was true, then the Lord of the universe, who created me and my unique personality, must have made a mistake. He must have misunderstood what I needed to be a great leader. He failed to hand me the tools I needed to be successful. He gave me a personality that wouldn't allow me to have a full life. The lesson I received from these two individuals was that my personality was going to set me up for floundering and not flourishing, for failure and not success.

But Psalm 139 makes me believe differently:

> You formed my inward parts;
>   you knitted me together in my mother's womb.
> I praise you, for I am fearfully and wonderfully made.
> Wonderful are your works;
>   my soul knows it very well. (verses 13–14)

If we believe Scripture to be true, then how could we conclude that God, who made us, does not have a plan for the uniqueness He knitted into every one of us? The simple truth is that God gave each of us a distinct personality and wired every person for a specific purpose. (As we delve more deeply into life-giving leadership, we will explore this passage as the basis on which to build our leadership.)

The light came on for me in the midst of a dark time, and I have spent the past decade trying to call out this truth in the lives of leaders. When the light clicks for people and they begin to become life-giving leaders by leading from their truest selves, their leadership explodes.

Unfortunately, we have all seen leaders take too long to grasp this principle. Because of their poor leadership, they lose valuable team members. Striving to understand your uniqueness and building confidence in your calling will last a lifetime. But the time to begin is now.

How Leadership and Faith Collide

I don't know anyone who walked away from his or her faith because of Jesus, but I know many who walked away because of the poor leadership of those who represent Jesus.

All of us are familiar with stories of Christian leaders who, because of self-centered decisions, have had moral failures involving finances, sex, or a multitude of other issues. And how about leaders who burn through staff members at a staggering rate, all in the pursuit of the mission? These leaders see their staff members as recruits—people who will do everything necessary to ensure their leaders achieve their desired level of recognition and honor.

What about leaders who choose to accept all the accolades for their team's hard work? When Christian leaders operate in a posture that benefits only them and not the people around them, it can inhibit and damage the faith of other people. We know the drill: our faith should be strong enough to survive the damage caused by another person's failures. That's easy to say, but it doesn't prevent bad leadership from driving people away from Jesus.

It doesn't matter whether you're a pastor or a librarian. If you are a follower of Jesus, I want you to feel the weight of this. We have probably all known someone who has walked away from faith because of another Christian's poor leadership. We must fight for our leadership to avoid this consequence.

I have dedicated myself to bringing hope to churches, organizations, nonprofits, and businesses. Christian leaders should be the best leaders in the world because we have the best Leader in history teaching us. We have the Creator infusing creativity into us. We have the Holy Spirit guiding us and giving us wisdom.

Great leadership demands that we stay in step with the Spirit. We need to learn the ways of life-giving leadership because it brings out the best in those around us as we lead from our truest selves. Look around. It's not hard to see the need for bringing life to others. You can do this only when you lead from your truest self, from your design. God created you for a purpose, which is to lead and to lead well.

Life-giving leaders carry the name of Jesus throughout communities and to the person standing next to them. They live out their calling with fulfillment and joy. They live to the fullest, just as Jesus implores us in John 10:10.

How we lead affects people's lives and their faith. That's a short sentence with an eternal impact. The weight of our leadership rests on our shoulders, and we need to carry it well. This is why I refer to the leadership that God calls us to as "life-giving." Here's what I mean.

Grace should flow from leaders to those around them. The most common type of leadership, however, is just the opposite. How many people have you worked for who required grace from their team members? Perhaps the leader was constantly late. Or maybe the leader lacked integrity, held unrealistic expectations, was an ineffective communicator, or was morally corrupt. We've all been there and never want to go back. Constantly having to give life and grace to those who lead you is exhausting. In contrast, wouldn't it be amazing to work for a leader who gives *you* life?

The best leader is one who continually extends grace rather than requiring it from others. The flow of grace is critical to the leader's ability to grow in influence. When leaders require grace to flow to them, the system is corrupt. It's backward. (Granted, as believers we are called to show grace and mercy to everyone, including bosses.)

Life-giving leadership flips the common scenario on its end. Life-giving leaders spread life, grace, hope, joy, and positivity like wildfire. The flow is consistent and contagious.

Rivers don't change direction because of a bad day. Unless something blocks the river, it will always flow in the same direction. Leaders who consistently change the flow of grace will lose influence.

WHEN LIFE FLOWS, INFLUENCE GROWS

The Colorado River, which created the Grand Canyon, is one of the most magnificent and powerful bodies of water in the United States. The Colorado, however, starts as a stream that you can straddle. La Poudre Pass is the simple beginning of this river whose beauty is known worldwide. If the Colorado River were to remain the size of where it begins its course, it would hardly make an impact. However, rivers grow as other streams join the flow. What starts small, barely attracting notice, can turn into one of the most powerful forces humanity has experienced.

Life-giving leadership can do the same. When leaders steward the small amount of influence they have in a God-honoring, life-giving way, it is no surprise when they are handed more influence and more opportunities to bring hope to others. Everyone has influence over someone. Great leadership involves stewarding or managing that influence over others to the best of our ability.

The world needs more life-giving leadership. Statistics indicate that more than 65 percent of working adults would choose a new boss over a pay increase.[1] Governments and politicians have lost influence, and the level of trust we place in other people tends to be lower now than in the past. The greatest management theories of our time are based on mistrust rather than trust. The path of mistrust leads to protecting investments, not pursuing greatness.

Many people would say the workplace is not a place where life is given but instead a place where life is taken. Management steals the joy from work and from workers. Team members live on their heels, constantly insecure because their leaders are managing them poorly.

I know this sounds bleak. It is bleak. But life-giving leadership changes the game. It brings color to monochrome organizations. It manifests light in dark places. It restores joy where joy has been lost. It pushes people to be their best. Who doesn't want to be known as a leader who does that?

Welcome to the lifelong pursuit of being a life-giving leader. You never arrive, but you get closer to the goal. Jack Nicklaus never stopped trying to improve his golf swing, even though he is considered the best of all time. Pablo Picasso never stopped trying to create his best masterpiece. William Shakespeare did not stop honing his craft after writing *Romeo and Juliet*.

Life-giving leaders will keep pursuing a better version of their leadership for the rest of their days. And trust me, *it's worth every minute.* If I were to ask people about the life-giving leaders they work with, I'm confident that they would say they are thankful for their leaders never quitting the race.

Writing this book was one aspect of my attempt to get better. I want to show others why life-giving leadership matters in this world that needs it so desperately. We are called to live a life worthy of the cross, to be salt and light in the world. We are commissioned to share the good news of Jesus with others, people in our offices and elsewhere. Evangelism is more than the words we say; it's the lives we live. We communicate the power of the Holy Spirit by the way He shows up in our day-to-day lives and in our leadership.

It is difficult to grasp the extent of the positive impact that life-giving leaders have on people. Better performance and a more productive work environment are a given, but the full extent of our impact comes about because we are called to live no other way.

WHAT TYPE OF LEADERS CAN BE LIFE GIVERS?

I have been asked if these principles apply only to leaders who call themselves Christian. The answer? The process of discovering your unique identity can apply to any leader. The truth that life-giving leaders bring life to those around them is applicable to everyone.

When I was in high school, I developed a relationship with Jesus. This was not merely attending church or acting religious or pretending to go along with the faith of my family; it was a true relationship with Christ. From that day on, I have pursued Him. As a teenager, I learned that two thousand years earlier Jesus died for me and my sins, He was resurrected from the dead, and He then offered me life. It was the most life-giving act the world has seen, and the world was never the same and I will never be the same.

This is 100 percent a Christian leadership book. I can't write about life-giving leadership without putting Jesus at the center of the conversation. He's the reason I can attempt to lead others to be their best. He's the reason I look my weaknesses square in the face and strive to improve. He's the reason I see every person on my team as a life-breathed version of our heavenly Father. Life-giving leadership is always filled with hope. So is Jesus. So is the gospel.

Leadership should be a radical reflection of the life that flows from God to us and then overflows from us to those around us. In keeping with that, you'll notice that this book is divided into four parts.

In this introductory section, we'll look at the calling of leadership on the lives of those who want to lead well. Why does leadership matter? What does great leadership look like? How does life-giving leadership change the game? And how will placing the principles of Jesus at the center of our leadership change the world? You will see that this divine directive is for you.

Part 1 dives deeply into how *you* matter in your leadership. The manner in which you lead comes from who you are. This section helps you look closely at your unique personality and leadership skills. You will see that God has wired you for your calling.

Part 2 might be the most difficult for some readers, and yet it is the most important section of this book. We cannot be the life-giving leaders God is calling us to be without learning and leading from our truest selves. We have to learn how to release the life givers within us. Have you ever met a great leader who was acting like someone he or she is not? This section will help you avoid the pitfalls of chasing other people's uniqueness and, instead, lead from your own strengths.

Part 3 shows practical ways that life-giving leaders lead daily. You will see why I believe the four *S*'s of leadership can serve as the basis for a lifetime of God-honoring leadership.

Finally, in part 4, you will learn how life-giving leaders change, and have an impact on, the businesses, churches, schools, and nonprofits they work for.

I pray that grace and life will flow from me to you and from God to you. I pray that you will see how life can flow from you and from your leadership.

When life flows, your influence grows. It's as simple as that, and yet it's never easy.

2

Divine Directive

You Are Divinely Called to Lead

My wife—Carrie—and I have two amazing boys, and I miss them when they're not with me. Watching them grow and mature is special. However, being a parent is the single most difficult and rewarding experience, involving the highest highs and lowest lows—from watching my kids learn to ride a bike to the nights when they just won't sleep (ugh).

And being a parent is not just *you* watching *them*. They also watch you. They see everything. They repeat everything, and because of that, they give a more accurate reflection than a mirror. For better or worse, they reflect the person you are. They are looking to see if what you do in your life is what you have told them to do.

It's the same with the world. People wonder if we leaders will do what we say and if our lives reflect what Scripture teaches. Whether married or single, parents or not, we will be followed very closely by the people around us.

A LEADER'S CALLING

Do you realize that you are called to be a life-giving leader? As followers of Jesus, we have been called by God to a higher standard in how we do life. He calls us to a standard that puts priority on His name, not ours. A standard that reflects the proper position for a follower of Jesus, which is a kingdom-first perspective.

Leaders, an epidemic of mediocre leadership plagues the world and the church today. I wish the church were protected from this issue, but it is not. Weak and damaging leadership hurts even more when it comes from those in the spiritual vocation. Even though I have suffered the harm of thoughtless leadership, I don't believe such leaders are intentionally malicious. I think they have instead seen it modeled so poorly they have no idea what healthy and effective leadership is.

After finishing seminary, I heard classmates talk about their call to preach the gospel. They discussed how much time they were devoting to preparing their weekly twenty-five-minute Sunday-morning messages. Preparation is essential, but you could spend hours on a message and still fail to connect with people. If you do not align your life and leadership with the words you speak on Sunday, all that preparation could be for naught.

If you believe the gospel can change lives and break chains but don't embrace that in your life as a leader, what does that say to the people under your leadership? In other words, do you show that you believe what you are teaching? Does the fruit of the truths you teach appear in your life and leadership first?

Or perhaps you work in the marketplace and observe poor leadership all around you. It's like a personal trainer who's out of shape. It's like a banker with a terrible financial portfolio. It's like a counselor with a long history of failed personal relationships who continues to tell paying clients what to do to save their marriages.

You've heard it said that doctors make the worst patients. It's the same dynamic with leaders. If you don't live out what you teach, you're not a true leader. If you truly believe your message brings life, why would you not let it transform your own life?

Author and pastor Andy Stanley said that "following Jesus will make your life better and make you better at life."[1] I would add that Jesus makes us better at leadership too. We believe the gospel brings life, so should we not also believe that a leader who accepts the divine directive from the Lord will be a life-giving leader—a leader who has life flowing from him or her?

A story in Ezekiel 47 gives a simple reminder of the flow of life. The prophet Ezekiel saw the ways the Lord wanted to restore Israel, bringing life back to the people He chose. Israel had lost hope, hence Ezekiel's vision of the valley of the dry bones found in chapter 37. The temple and the city of Jerusalem were in ruins. Hope and life were far from the minds of most of the people of Israel.

Then the prophet came to a temple that had a river flowing from underneath, and that is where the Lord walked with Ezekiel.

> He led me back to the bank of the river. As I went back, I saw on the bank of the river very many trees on the one side and on the other. And he said to me, "This water flows toward the eastern region and goes down into the Arabah, and enters the sea; when the water flows into the sea, the water will become fresh. And wherever the river goes, every living creature that swarms will live, and there will be very many fish. For this water goes there, that the waters of the sea may become fresh; *so everything will live where the river goes.* Fishermen will stand beside the sea. From Engedi to Eneglaim it will be a place for the spreading of nets. Its fish will be of very many kinds, like the fish of the Great Sea. . . . And on the banks, on both sides of the river, there will grow all kinds of trees for food. Their leaves will not wither, nor their fruit fail, but they

will bear fresh fruit every month, because the water for them flows from the sanctuary. Their fruit will be for food, and their leaves for healing." (verses 6–10, 12)

This stands in dramatic contrast to what the people were experiencing. Here, life was flowing from the temple. In the Old Testament, the temple was regarded as the dwelling place of God. So the image of the river flowing from the Lord should not be hard to envision. In this hard season of the history of God's people, God wanted to paint a new picture. Life flowed from the Lord to the creatures in the river, which in turn brought life and sustenance to fishermen. Even those near the water received life from the river.

Don't miss this important phrasing—that "the water for *them* flows from the sanctuary." It was flowing in that direction—outward from God's dwelling place—because the people needed it.

Leaders, let's allow this picture to help us understand our calling. Our divine directive is to lead well because we are to send life from us to other people. When we lead poorly, life flows in the wrong direction. If we don't allow life to flow outward, those who need the proper flow will not receive it.

HOW YOU LEAD AFFECTS PEOPLE'S FAITH

I've mentioned this before and I hope you're getting the point. The pronoun is critical—I want you to think of *you*. People's faith is affected by how *you* lead and serve. In any setting: marketplace or ministry, nonprofit or for-profit. I realize this is a lot of pressure and it should be.

You can make a perfectly right decision, but if you address it in the wrong way, you are no longer right. As a Jesus follower, and even more so as a church staff member, you could derail someone's faith journey by mishandling a situation.

I have a close friend who is one of the most generous people I know. I love and appreciate him for who he is. We share some similarities, especially when it comes to our ability to talk. All the time. We might even cross the line with sarcasm occasionally.

My friend was active in our church, and it's not an exaggeration to say the church changed his life. He talks about how he had previously known about God but didn't know Jesus. He had no relationship with Jesus before coming to the church. My friend's life and faith were ignited by this new relationship.

My friend has no pretense; he always is himself. You don't have to guess who he is or what kind of person he is. It's right there in front of you. After he became a Jesus follower, his gregarious personality remained the same while Jesus continued to change his heart. His faith was taking on a life of its own, which affected every aspect of his world.

Until one Sunday morning.

At church that morning, my friend made a comment that was unintentionally off-color. The comment was inappropriate and he realized it. He caught himself and apologized immediately.

The bad news? Even though my friend made a mistake and acted quickly to do what he could to make it right, it was too late. He had the self-awareness to know that a Jesus follower should not make the comment he'd made. He was humble enough to admit it, to openly apologize.

Still, it wasn't enough.

Self-awareness allows us to recognize our actions, our words, our attitudes, and our behavior. It is a gatekeeper between our minds and our mouths. A joke or other comment might come to mind, but self-awareness tells us it's not appropriate. Self-regulation helps us leave it unspoken. That internal gatekeeper gets our attention and tells us to stop *before* we make an inappropriate, untimely, or hurtful comment.

Self-awareness is a necessary component of emotional intelligence. My talkative, Jesus-loving friend had failed to exercise this aspect of emotional intelligence to monitor his comments. One statement he made on a Sunday morning caused much distress and distrust. Feelings were hurt and both my friend and the offended party were in a tough spot. Ultimately, my friend was asked to take a break from volunteering at church.

It was a really difficult situation, and I might've made the same decision to give him a break from serving. Do you know how hard it is to ask an enthusiastic volunteer to step down? Extremely hard. They serve for free, for crying out loud! Nonetheless, a leader has to consider the lives of other people as he or she considers the effect of one individual. So the decision to have my friend's serving go on hiatus was probably a life-giving decision.

But in leadership you can make a perfectly right decision while handling it in the wrong way. When that happens, you are no longer right.

That was the case with my friend's situation. Asking him to take a break from serving was probably the right decision, but it was managed carelessly. Basically, the leader jumped to conclusions without talking to both sides—my friend and the offended party. Without hearing the whole story, the leader called my friend and removed him from his position. There was no conversation about what had happened.

It was handled so poorly that my friend went into a two-year faith spiral. He didn't enter our church once during that time. It was painful to watch, and there wasn't much I could do. We still had conversations about faith. We still talked about life, business, and family, but he stayed home on Sundays.

Many pastors and leaders on a church staff never understand or embrace how important their leadership is to the faith of their congregation. They might embrace their callings to preach, counsel, teach, serve children, and so forth, but they never embrace that they are *leaders*. The people they serve see them as representatives of Jesus and of faith in Jesus. In fact, most followers of Jesus (pastors, laypersons, managers, employees) don't recognize the impact their leadership has on the faith of others. More simply put, we are called to manage our influence on others in light of what Jesus said is the most important priority.

A religious leader asked, "Teacher, which is the greatest commandment in the Law?"

And look how Jesus replied:

"Love the Lord your God with all your heart and with all your soul and with all your mind." This is the first and greatest commandment. And the second is like it: "Love your neighbor as yourself." (Matthew 22:36–39, NIV)

Life-giving leadership is all about staying in deep relationship with our heavenly Father so we can love those around us best and bring life to the people God has put in our circle of influence. A driving force behind this book is to help believers fully realize the importance of leadership to every follower of Jesus.

DIVINE DIRECTIVE

As followers of Jesus and representatives of the gospel, we are given a standard of leadership different from that of the world. It's a higher standard that governs how we treat people, a better version of how to invest in those around us. We have been given a divine directive to lead well. God calls us to change the world by the power of His truth and the gospel that is lived out through our leadership. Leaders who understand this begin to bring life to the community they serve.

Think of your family, your boyfriend or girlfriend, your coworkers, and the volunteers in your organization. You represent God to every one of these people, and for that reason I want you to be aware of life-giving leadership. In short, *how you lead affects people's faith.* I mention this again because we can't possibly lead people well if we fail to recognize this.

What if the greatest gift you can give your church is great leadership? What if the most spiritual thing you can do this week is to lead the people around you well? To do that, you first need to embrace your call to lead, because failing to do so would be like assuming your money will do what's best for you without your first creating a financial plan. To be a life-giving leader requires accepting the power and calling on your life to lead and then developing plans for leading well.

What It Means to Be Called

Calling probably ranks in the top five most googled faith searches. Who doesn't want to know what God is calling them to do?

Here's a story that helps shift calling from a theory or concept to ground-level living. It also sheds light on what it means to lead well as a life-giving leader.

My two amazing boys bring a crazy amount of fun, laughter, sports, and life to our family. Being their dad is one of the greatest gifts I could ever ask for. Over the years, my wife and I have developed a system for communication while I'm at work. If she calls once and I don't answer, she knows I'm probably in a meeting (which is usually true). If there's an emergency, however, she will call back immediately.

About a week after our youngest son was born, I was trying to get back into the swing of work. Having a newborn at home is brutal on your sleep schedule, so my wife and I came up with a great plan. When it was time for his late-night feeding, I would get out of bed and get him ready for my wife to feed him. Then I'd go back to sleep. But when newborn children are involved, even the greatest plan in the world can't guarantee any extra sleep. In fact, I remember very little from the first six weeks with either of my boys because I was so tired. It was an amazing time, but it was extremely hard!

The week following each birth was no exception to the normal pattern of parental sleep deprivation and adjustment. In spite of that, it was back to work as usual after just a few days off.

At the time, I was working with Andy Stanley at North Point Ministries. I was the service programming director (SPD) at the Browns Bridge campus. Every Tuesday, the SPDs from the different campuses would meet with Andy to work through the upcoming sermon series and the Sunday program for that week. This particular week was no different, except I was desperately trying to stay awake.

About twenty minutes into the meeting, I received a phone call from my wife. I politely declined the call (which you do when it's your wife) and put the phone back in my pocket. Then the phone rang again.

Let me stop the story for a second. It would not have mattered if I were in the Oval Office for a meeting with the president. I would still have answered my phone. If I were at the Vatican, hanging out with the pope, I would have excused myself to take the call. If I had been at Augusta National and my wife was calling a second time, I'd like to think I would have dropped everything and taken the call. I'm mostly kidding about the last one, but you understand what I'm trying to say. There is no higher priority to me than answering the phone when that second call comes in.

So at the meeting with the other SPDs, I excused myself to answer the phone. My mother-in-law told me my wife had experienced a postdelivery medical emergency. I'm so thankful for our priority-message system. Her call took precedence over everything else and everyone else.

Not a thing in the world would have been more important than that call. As a leader and a believer, what are the things you consider priorities, the things that come ahead of *everything* else?

For followers of Jesus, the divine directive to lead well for God's glory should sit at the top of our lists. Many of you will read this and think, *That's a little extreme, don't you think? Leadership is really* that *high a call?* The answer is yes.

Do I think the preeminence of the divine directive applies to all believers, not just pastors? Yes, I do.

What It Costs to Be Called

I encourage you to embrace the level of calling that takes precedence over all else. When you represent Jesus, your leadership could be one of the most critical ways people see your faith lived out. More importantly, many people will determine how to integrate faith into their lives based on how you lead. I want you to feel the weight of your leadership as well as the impact it will make on the people around you.

If we are to bring life to those around us, we *have* to lead from this place of calling! There is no other way. The leaders who change the world have chosen to embrace this calling. The reason this is mission-critical for believers is because the fate of many hangs in the balance. Eternity. We are to be men and women who reflect our heavenly Father and show others a glimpse of what's to come. It is an all-in situation. You can't be a life-giving leader without being all-in. This is not a pursuit for the faint of heart. It's hard. It brings tears and heartbreak.

Yet life-giving leaders make the people around them shine. They create places filled with leaders who have shiny eyes as well as leaders who feel loved and operate from a place of fullness and joy. Shiny eyes show hope, passion, and excitement. The mission is worth the pain, the challenge, and the striving. Just ask the mother of a newborn if the pain of the journey was worth it.

The joy and fun our boys bring to our family are unreal. The pain and craziness they bring are also unreal, but we would not change a thing. The pain endured by my wife to give our sons life and to bring them into this world has never made her question whether it was worth it. We are thankful for the pain, because without it, we would not have two of the most amazing people this world has ever seen.

In my work as a leader for the past twenty years, every episode of hardship, pain, and frustration has been worth it. I have experienced heart-break when leaders left for new opportunities after I had invested in them for years. I have suffered the pain of watching others make mistakes and pain from making my own mistakes.

But then a day comes when the people I have led choose to make life-giving decisions. They give life to those around them. They have learned to make wise decisions, and they create a new space that grows leaders. They show incredible creativity and innovation that builds new products. When these things happen, we are reminded that leading others is well worth the investment. Life-giving leadership is not without its rewards.

I have watched team members show up for work early and stay late to serve a person on their team. I have seen them give life by writing notes to individuals around them as a way to love people in a unique way. I've watched leaders have hard but loving conversations with their own leaders because it will serve their leaders better in the long run. Anyone can try to lead. But to be life-giving leaders, we often have to put ourselves in a tough spot to move another person and the interpersonal relationship further by coaching the person through his or her struggle.

I'll say it again: life-giving leadership is a divine directive and it requires sacrifice. Jesus talked about sacrifice in Mark 8:

> Calling the crowd to join his disciples, he said, "Anyone who intends to come with me has to let me lead. You're not in the driver's seat; I am. Don't run from suffering; embrace it. Follow me and I'll show you how. Self-help is no help at all. Self-sacrifice is the way, my way, to saving yourself, your true self. What good would it do to get everything you want and lose you, the real you? What could you ever trade your soul for?" (verses 34–37, MSG)

Choosing to put others before yourself is life-giving leadership. It involves following Jesus by never divorcing how you lead from your faith.

I've watched some leaders who were Jesus followers leave their faith at the door when they came to the office. That's not an option when you have received the divine directive. How you treat people is based on the belief that, in every interaction, you are eyeball-to-eyeball with someone who has value. Someone Jesus died for.

Other than Jesus, there is nothing of higher value in my life than my family. They are worth the pursuit. They are worth the joys and sorrows. They are worth anything that might be required of me.

So are the leaders God has entrusted to you and me. They deserve our best in training, mentoring, trust, and grace. They deserve our leadership in freeing them to lead. They deserve our love and our life. They deserve the investment of a life-giving leader.

Our best should be reserved for the best things: our families, our friends, and our God. When we place these three in proper focus and priority, we see that life makes more sense. It becomes clearer and the people around us take notice.

One of the most attractive elements of life-giving leaders is that they know what they are about and who they are when at their best. Usually, it's when they are leading others. They give others their best, and that's life-giving leadership.

By now you know it matters. Let's lean in and see what it takes to become this type of leader.

Part 1

Leading from Your Truest Self

Leadership matters. That's how I would sum up part 1. It matters because all leadership affects people, and we know that people matter. They are why we do what we do. One of the consistent charges I give to my team at Catalyst is to maintain this perspective: people are not an interruption to our day; they *are* our day.

It's not just that others matter; it's that *you* matter. You matter especially to your leadership. It's your leadership, for goodness' sake. You are a steward of the amazing personality-and-gift set God has entrusted to you. He gave you a brain, instincts, organization, and many other gifts to grow your leadership and the kingdom.

Without *you,* your leadership is nonexistent. I know people who possessed tremendous potential as leaders, but they never became comfortable with themselves. As a result, they never came close to realizing the potential of their calling, their giftedness, and their opportunities.

In this section, you will discover why *you* are so important to your leadership. I didn't just make this up. It has been true for thousands of years. God was up to something when He made you. He was up to something amazing.

3

No Regrets

Life-Giving Leaders Lead
from Their Truest Selves

Have you ever known individuals who changed who they were in an attempt to fit the expectations of those around them? If no one comes to mind, think back to middle school or high school when way too many of us adapted who we were or who we wanted to be just to fit in.

For me, the year was 1989. I was a muscular eighth grader. Okay. I'm from the South and we are pretty good at exaggerating. I weighed eighty-five pounds and had an amazing haircut that was spiked right down the middle. (It was similar to the soccer mullet from back in the day, but I didn't have the waterfall in the back.)

I was interested in being stylish, but I'm not sure I knew how to pull it off. My parents made sure I had nice clothes, but I wouldn't say I really knew what style I wanted to follow. Preppy? Sporty? Grunge? As I tell my own story, I know there's not a former middle schooler out there who hasn't gone through a similar scenario of trying to figure it out.

One of my favorite figuring-it-out moments came in the form of an eighth-grade social. It was a dance. With girls. In my middle-school prime, I was a good ten inches shorter than my buddies. (I was a late bloomer.) I weeded through the long line of girls who were begging to be my date and settled on a neighborhood friend. Now for the hard part: deciding what to wear.

No longer would I be a middle schooler without a style. This was the moment. I was going to be a new man, which meant there was only one article of clothing that would take me to a whole new level in my progression into puberty: Z. Cavariccis.

Let me get the millennials up to speed. Z. Cavariccis were the jam. Brand name on the zipper. High sides on the hips. Tight rolled at the bottom. They were lady-killers.

They were also the most expensive item of clothing I had ever owned. It was a sacrifice for my parents but not for me. These slacks were going to be a game changer.

When I entered the school cafeteria for the eighth-grade social, the place looked like a scene from *Napoleon Dynamite*. I knew this was my moment of glory, except for two key things.

1. Every other guy there had on the same pants. (Ugh.)
2. The pants were incredibly uncomfortable. A lot like stepping-on-a-Lego-at-night uncomfortable.

They were uncomfortable because they were not me.

As soon as I got home, I changed into something else. I needed to get back to being myself. Isn't it exhausting to try to keep up an appearance that's not you simply because you think other people will find you cool or attractive?

I know this is a silly example, but let's play it out in our adult lives. Have you ever attempted to act a certain way at work because a number of your colleagues acted that way? Have you ever felt pressured to sacrifice your values because "that's just business"?

I guess a bigger question is this: Have you ever felt as if you were able to be your truest self at work? Do you appreciate the uniqueness of those around you? What would it do to your motivation to be fully yourself instead of fully what you think you're supposed to be? Do you feel alive while you are leading?

Just as a man-made dam or a landslide causes rivers to stop flowing correctly, when leaders choose to lead from any place but their truest selves, life flow can be cut off. When leaders use practices or pursuits untrue to who they are, the flow of life can be blocked or diverted. When you don't lead from your truest self, you are blocked from serving others to your fullest potential.

A Change of Pace and Direction

Bronnie Ware was tired of working jobs that weren't fulfilling. She started working in hospice care and something beautiful happened, as it often does when one chooses to serve others. Her clients in hospice changed her life. Life started becoming clearer for her as she listened to those at the end of theirs.

In 2009 Bronnie wrote about the regrets of men and women coming to the end of their time on earth. She would sit alongside people as they reflected on their lives and prepared for the inevitable.

When I read her article, I was shocked and overwhelmed by the number one regret. I would have put money on the fact that the second most frequently mentioned regret (that they worked too hard) would have claimed the number one spot. But that was not the most consistent response.

Here is the top regret, as described in Bronnie Ware's article:

When questioned about any regrets they had or anything they would do differently, common themes surfaced again and again. . . .

1. I wish I'd had the courage to live a life true to myself, not the life others expected of me.

This was the most common regret of all. When people realise that their life is almost over and look back clearly on it, it is easy to see how many dreams have gone unfulfilled. Most people had not honoured even a half of their dreams and had to die knowing that it was due to choices they had made, or not made.[1]

Think about the number one regret. *I wasn't my truest self.*

Leaders, this cannot be our story. These dying men and women have opened our eyes to this truth. Please make sure you heed their warning. We will dive deeply into the process of defining and leaning into our God-given uniqueness. We will settle for nothing less than leading from our purest selves.

ABUNDANT LIVING AND LEADING

Jesus didn't become central to my life until late in high school. Growing up, I was around church, but I never had a relationship with Jesus. The concept we've been talking about—how leaders who represent Jesus affect the faith of others—is central to my story.

First, an insight into my personality. I'm not a deep person. My lowest-ranking love language is quality time.[2] My wife's highest-ranking love language is, of course, quality time. Our love language difference could be a book in itself, but back to the point. I really am okay, at times, with no deep conversation. I'm fine with small talk and chatting. I can go there if necessary, and we all have to move in and out of our primary strengths and preferences to experience abundant life. But I don't need much quality time to fill my bucket!

Now I'll display my simple thinking: when I was in high school, I pretty much just wanted to have fun. If it wasn't fun, I wasn't interested. The truth is that even now, not much has changed. I still want to have fun.

I didn't know anyone who was a consistent follower of Jesus who lived free and had fun. I know that's a massive overstatement. But for a sixteen-year-old, it was a big deal. I knew enough about the Bible to know that being a Jesus follower would require some sacrifice of behavior and a different posture in the world. Why would I sign up for that if it meant giving up on fun?

Then I was invited by some really close friends to go to a youth group. I had never seen anything like it. These students loved Jesus, and—get this—they were having fun. Didn't they realize that Christianity was supposed to be stuffy, dressed up, boring, and only applicable on Sundays? I could not wrap my head around this fun-and-faith phenomenon.

In the midst of my brain exploding with curiosity, they invited me to a Christian concert. To this day I can recall the moment I looked around during the show and saw this light in people. Joy. Smiles. And fun. They were having fun, and it was centered on Jesus. It was too good to be true, and it changed me forever.

"I came that they may have life and have it abundantly" (John 10:10) became my favorite verse in the Bible. It has been central to my life and leadership for the past twenty-five years. This simple verse should bring all of us so much gratitude and joy. Jesus didn't die for us so we could live trapped, boring, broken lives. He didn't teach that abundant life can happen only after you get it together or when you mature into the person He wants you to be. He talks of living to the fullest now, while you're becoming the person you want to be and He wants you to be.

Neither did Jesus die so you could work hard at being someone else. He died for the *you* that God knit together. That's who Jesus loves: you. That's who He wants to have a life filled with joy and abundance: you.

Toward the end of this book, we'll look at how this concept plays out in organizations. How life-giving leaders bring color to monochrome places. For now, though, I would bet God might be stirring in you. He might well be reminding you of a season of life when you were alive. He might be refreshing your mind with what abundant life looks like.

As I'm writing this, I'm in Montana, sitting on a porch overlooking the Bighorn River. Breathing in this clean air and overlooking God's creation, I can feel this concept more than I have in a while. And as I mention this, I get it. I know that life comes at you at the speed of light. It often requires that you push through a season of too many demands, too many needs, and too much chaos. However, we have to pursue refreshment and refueling to have something to give to others.

I believe we can not only live this abundant life but also lead from a place of abundance. When you are filled with abundant life, it will overflow to those you lead. It has to. When you are leading from a place of emptiness, it's tough to let life flow from you. It's difficult to muster up the energy to pour yourself out when you are already tapped out.

Leaders, you cannot give what you do not have. If you are depleted of life and grace, you cannot give it. It will not flow from you, and you cannot have a lasting influence without consistent flow.

CONNECTED TO THE SOURCE

No-regrets leadership requires an abundant-life mentality. An all-in, everyday-counts type of posture. As we have discussed, it also requires leaders to have a reservoir of life to give to others. The entire concept of life-giving leaders is built on having something to give. Jesus created a simple yet profound visual of how we are to do this. You cannot give away what you don't have. Rivers without water are no longer rivers. Leaders without life flowing into them cannot be life-giving leaders.

This is how Jesus presented it: "I am the true vine, and my Father is the vinedresser. . . . Abide in me, and I in you. As the branch cannot bear fruit by itself, unless it abides in the vine, neither can you, unless you abide in me. I am the vine; you are the branches. Whoever abides in me and I in him, he it is that bears *much* fruit, for apart from me you can do nothing" (John 15:1, 4–5).

I know many of you have heard this passage a million times, but I want you to hear it again.

"Apart from me you can do nothing." A branch without a vine ceases to exist. It never has the possibility to form. And without branches, the vine has nothing to show. The vine-branch relationship needs both parties. In this teaching, Jesus is emphasizing the importance of being connected.

As Jesus followers, we must be connected to the Source of life, the Vine. You can't just stick a branch in the ground and expect it to have life. The branch is designed to bear fruit, and it can't do that without being connected to the Vine.

This is the basis of life-giving leadership. If we're not connected to Jesus, and if we're not connected to one another, life will never flow from the leader to other people. A river needs to be connected to the spring that is its source. A tree must be rooted in the soil to receive water and nutrients. Otherwise, instead of flourishing, it will die. And if you forget to recharge your mobile devices the night before, they won't last the day. If you want to develop into a life-giving leader, you have to be connected to the power source, which in our case is the Source of life.

If you think you can flourish as a leader without this, you're wrong. Life-giving leadership can come only from a place of overflow, a place of abundance, a place characterized by fruit.

Our lives will be filled with regret if we aren't filled with life. So many of us lead others even though our lives are depleted and dry wells, empty of grace. In a later chapter we will talk about the importance of a leader's health. It's not optional to be healthy. It's crucial.

To be what we were designed to be, the components need to all be in place. Abundant life and fruit give evidence of the goodness of the Source.

Without a connection to our heavenly Father through the connection of Jesus, we will dry up. And with that, we will miss our purpose.

How do we live out what we were designed for? What does that look like? Where do we turn? And as leaders, don't we all have to compromise at times? The key is to grasp one of the most important elements of life-giving leadership, which is *you*. By that I mean the person God created you to be, with all your uniqueness, your gifts, and your specially designed fruit.

When we discover how to live and how to lead as the person God made each of us to be, we will live our lives in a way few people experience.

No regrets.

$$\underline{4}$$

Made Especially for Leadership

Life-Giving Leaders Embrace
Their Uniqueness

I have a problem. Every year I start playing Christmas music before Thanksgiving, and I don't care who knows it.

I play all the classics and all the new songs. Even "Dominick the Italian Christmas Donkey" brings joy to my heart. But one song stands above all others. One song by one artist changes the game every year. I get giddy just anticipating Celine Dion's rendition of "O Holy Night." When she hits that high note, you wonder if Jesus might have been waiting for it so He can come back.

Have you ever seen Celine Dion in concert? Me neither. (By the way, unless it's late in the year, I don't drive around listening to Celine. But if you are a year-round fan, more power to you.) Even though she's not a regular on my car radio, I understand that she was *made* to sing. Rumor has it her live show brings tears to your eyes. To do that, you have to be made for it.

We need to understand that how something is made points to its unique design, and the unique design correlates with its purpose. If you have seen a master guitarist perform, you understand this concept. Not only do you have to understand time signatures, chord progressions, variations in volume, key signatures, and much more having to do with music theory, you also have to learn how to tune the guitar. Without a properly tuned guitar, the best musicians in the world can't make the instrument sound right. Before audience members can recognize the melody, the guitarist has to master a basic understanding of how the guitar was made to be played.

The same is true, of course, for any instrumentalist. But most saxophone players won't know where to begin if they're handed a guitar. The beauty of a guitar's sound comes from an understanding of its purpose and possibilities. It was designed and crafted to be played in a specific way. And the best guitars reflect the work of master builders. Taylor Guitars, for example, carry a patent on their state-of-the-art guitar neck. The neck and the neck joint are engineered to enhance beautiful sound.

So were you. You are the most important part of your leadership. God created living beings with a purpose. A bird was made to fly, and a shark was made to swim. They were woven together for unique reasons and purposes. You were made to lead, and the pathway to giving away the most life is to lead according to the way you were created.

You Were Made to Lead

As a follower of Jesus, I see Scripture as a gift from the Lord. Jesus believed the Old Testament was true, and as pastor and author Andy Stanley has said, "Anyone who can predict their own death and resurrection and pull it off . . . I'll believe what they believe."

I agree with Jesus, the apostle Paul, and King David of ancient Israel: Scripture is a gift from God. David's contribution to the canon includes songs from his heart. We read his words in songs of pain, songs of love, songs of understanding and misunderstanding, songs of beauty and fear. In David's writings we are given permission to speak honestly with God. We are also given glimpses into God's indescribable goodness and majesty.

David is recognized as one of the greatest leaders of ancient Israel, and today the greatest leaders in the world have figured out that great leadership is faith-based leadership. Our trust in God's Word solidifies our understanding of life, ourselves, leadership, and especially faith-based leadership.

If you are not sure about faith, the authority of the Bible, and God's call on leaders, keep reading, because principles here will help you in your leadership. As a matter of fact, many times people quote Bible verses without knowing it. The Golden Rule of do unto others as you want done unto you is in the New Testament. One of the often quoted books in the Old Testament is the book of Psalms, which contains the writings of David that lay the foundation for life-giving leadership. If you believe Scripture was given to us by our Creator, then we need to connect His love and His belief in us with our leadership.

Read the first part of this amazing passage.

GOD, investigate my life;
   get all the facts firsthand.
I'm an open book to you;
   even from a distance, you know what I'm thinking.
You know when I leave and when I get back;
   I'm never out of your sight.
You know everything I'm going to say
   before I start the first sentence.
I look behind me and you're there,
   then up ahead and you're there, too—
   your reassuring presence, coming and going.

This is too much, too wonderful—
   I can't take it all in!

Is there anyplace I can go to avoid your Spirit?
   to be out of your sight?
If I climb to the sky, you're there!
   If I go underground, you're there!
If I flew on morning's wings
   to the far western horizon,
You'd find me in a minute—
   you're already there waiting!
Then I said to myself, "Oh, he even sees me in the dark!
   At night I'm immersed in the light!"
It's a fact: darkness isn't dark to you;
   night and day, darkness and light, they're all the same to you.
     (Psalm 139:1–12, MSG)

What a wonderful thought that you can't leave God's Spirit! If you are pursuing God, it's a comforting truth. It can be a scary thought if you are running from God. If you are far from God and living in places you don't want people to know about, the idea that God is there is crazy. Where you are is the last place you want to see Him.

However, when you are in need of God, He is there. You don't have to search. You don't have to figure it out. He's there, living inside you. He is with you when you lead and when you choose not to lead.

David was overwhelmed by this incredible idea, and we should be as well. It is an "amazing grace" story of God staying with us. By the way, it gets even better. This next passage gives me continued hope that God has a unique plan in my life and leadership. Listen to David's beautiful reminder of God's design of every person.

Oh yes, you shaped me first inside, then out;
  you formed me in my mother's womb.
I thank you, High God—you're breathtaking!
  Body and soul, I am marvelously made!
  I worship in adoration—what a creation!
You know me inside and out,
  you know every bone in my body;
You know exactly how I was made, bit by bit,
  how I was sculpted from nothing into something.
Like an open book, you watched me grow from conception to
    birth;
  all the stages of my life were spread out before you,
The days of my life all prepared
  before I'd even lived one day. (Psalm 139:13–16, MSG)

God formed you. Let that sink in. As I write this, I'm pausing to ponder that thought. God formed me. Whoa.

That deserves taking a break from reading and spending some time on our knees in worship. "Thank You, Lord, for making us. Thank You, Lord, for creating Your children in Your image. Even in our uniqueness, we bear Your image. Even in our peculiarities and fears, we reflect our Creator's work. Thank You."

David wrote, "You shaped me first inside, then out." Do you believe that? Let me ask you, When was the last time you didn't like something about your personality? When was the last time you found yourself believing the lies Satan told you about yourself? The Accuser wants nothing more than for you to believe that God did not shape you "first inside, then out." Satan wants to convince you that you were and are a mistake, that the way you're wired doesn't matter, that you should change who you are to match someone else's gifts and talents because yours aren't good enough.

If your attention is waning, stop and read this truth again. "You shaped me first inside, then out; you formed me in my mother's womb." If we believe God's truth is for us, and if we agree Scripture was given to us by our Father in heaven, then we have to take this passage seriously. This might be the most freeing thing you've read in years. I can tell you this passage changed my leadership forever. Psalm 139 allowed me to take the moment when I was told I wouldn't be successful because of my personality and use it to become a better person and leader. I realized that my calling and purpose can be fully reached only through my uniqueness.

We were made by God for God. I don't believe God would make us in a certain way and then expect us to live and lead in another way. Our Designer molded every one of us with His purposes in mind.

King David's life story documents the glory of being chosen as king of Israel as well as moments of horrible decision-making. His mistakes were broadcast across the kingdom. But he also made incredibly wise decisions, such as not to kill his failed predecessor, Saul, even though he had plenty of opportunities.

The same David who worshipped God without hindrance is the David who ran from God and then returned to Him. He is the same David who wrote, "All the stages of my life were spread out before you." He is the same David who called on the courage infused into our souls to defeat Goliath.[1] David, the former shepherd boy named king, believed that before he was born, God knit him together with the scope of his life in view.

Leaders, you were made uniquely for a unique purpose. Your design and your leadership can't be separated. There is no question we have to continue growing as leaders; we have to continue to get better. But the core of who we were created to be has to stay intact and connected to our growth. This book is all about growth, but it has to be growth from the core, growth based on the truth that God formed us. God didn't make a mistake when He didn't give you the talent you covet in someone else. We will reject the lie that any of us was designed in error. Instead, we will believe that God is the greatest designer.

If you need an impressive reminder of this, think about your eyes.

THE DESIGN OF YOUR EYES

The eye is composed of more than two million working parts. More than one million nerve fibers connect each eye to the brain, and they can't be reconstructed. A fingerprint has 40 unique characteristics, but the iris of the eye has 256, which is one of the reasons retina scans are increasingly being used for security purposes.

Even our eyelids demonstrate God's design. Eyelids protect our eyes from dust and debris. Tears don't just clean our eyes; they also contain antimicrobial agents that help us feel better after crying emotional tears. And get this—the focusing muscles in your eyes move approximately one hundred thousand times a day. To give your leg muscles the same workout, you'd need to walk fifty miles. And it's not just the physical makeup of eyes that shows the intentionality behind them but also the way they work with other parts of the body. Eighty percent of our memories are determined by what we see, and our eyes are the second most complex organs, after the brain.[2]

The body is a perfect example of the partnership between design and purpose, creation and function. All parts work together so we can conquer the smallest feats, such as blinking an eye. The parts also work together so we can claim larger conquests, such as running a marathon or giving birth. It's fascinating.

Just as our bodies can't function without all the intricate details God created working together, we can't become the leaders and Christ followers God made us to be until we walk in full acceptance of and confidence in how He wired us.

All the parts of your personality and your leadership—even the things you wish you could change—are intentional. They are designed for *your* purpose. You can't function at your best as a leader without the involvement of each part of you that makes you who you are.

You are a combination of untold numbers of fearfully and wonderfully made details. God did not take a shortcut when He made you. You were designed to lead as the person He made you to be.

This is how David saw the mind of God:

> Your thoughts—how rare, how beautiful!
>   God, I'll never comprehend them!
> I couldn't even begin to count them—
>   any more than I could count the sand of the sea.
> Oh, let me rise in the morning and live always with you!
>   And please, God, do away with wickedness for good!
>   (Psalm 139:17–19, MSG)

What a song of worship! I'm sure we all think we can do some things better than God can. We think we have a better understanding of timing. Often we find ourselves giving God advice on when our circumstances should change.

Maybe it's not timing you feel you know more about. What if you feel God should have put you in other relationships or in a better job? What about the times I think God missed a detail when He made me an unstructured person and I see again and again that the world loves structured people?

Okay, I'll tell you. I wonder why I'm so unstructured when I struggle to focus beyond that last sentence. Meanwhile, the world around me is already charging on to the next accomplishment. Or what about the fact that I'm about as extroverted as they come but I regularly see that being overly extroverted rubs some people the wrong way?

I've wrestled with the same questions you wrestle with. I'm often overwhelmed by the feeling that I'm inadequate. Plus I tend to believe that if I possessed certain gifts I've noticed in other people that things would improve in my current situation. The reality is we can't understand why God made us exactly as He did. Only God understands that. And we will never come up with better timing on things than God's timing. His plans are great (see Jeremiah 29:11), and His original plan for how He created you is no exception.

Don't Doubt That God Has the Best Plan

David worshipped God by saying he never wanted to be separated from God's thinking. Nor do I. When we leaders stop trusting God's sovereignty over our lives, we have put ourselves in His position. God is God and we're not. We could never pull off doing anything better than God can.

David concluded his song of worship with an invitation to God.

> Investigate my life, O God,
> find out everything about me;
> Cross-examine and test me,
> get a clear picture of what I'm about;
> See for yourself whether I've done anything wrong—
> then guide me on the road to eternal life.
> (Psalm 139:23–24, MSG)

Search me, then guide me.

Our heavenly Father made us beautifully. He knows you, and He knows how to lead you best. We're not God, so we have flaws. There are areas in which we need to grow. And life-giving leaders understand we can't use our uniqueness as a crutch to keep from growing.

How many leaders do you know who are highly verbal? We all know some. But how many of these leaders have you heard say, "Well, that's just me. I shoot straight with people"? Shooting straight is great when it refers to a leader's integrity, honesty, and lack of pretense. But when it means stating what's on your mind with no filter, it's almost always harmful.

A life-giving leader knows that emotional intelligence plays a crucial role in communication. When shooting straight means speaking before thinking, leaders lose influence. I've said I'm a naturally unstructured person. But that doesn't allow me to be terrible at communication, nor does it mean I can stop working to get the details in order. I'll probably never be great when it comes to details, but I will always try to improve.

Search me, God. Then guide me.

Leaders, who you are is quite possibly the most important element in your leadership. It is your leadership, after all, not the leadership of someone else. You cannot lead from someone else's seat. The catcher doesn't pitch. But he is a superb catcher.

I recently had a retreat with my key leadership team. I enjoy few things more than seeing how perfectly a person is suited to accomplishing a specific task. When a new project comes up, the team chooses who will take point for that project. It takes little to no effort to settle on the best leader because we know one another well. We know the person that each of us is, so finding the best fit between person and project comes fairly easily.

Knowing yourself and your staff members well is essential in other areas. When you operate more than half the time out of learned behavior rather than internally determined behavior, you will be exhausted because you are trying to be something you are not. You are working outside of your natural gifting and wiring.

And before you send me emails about paying your dues and doing whatever it takes to get the job done, let me help you understand where I'm coming from. Every one of us has to do things we don't like doing. Even when you sit at the top of the org chart, you will be required to make certain things happen whether you like them or not. A leader doesn't shirk responsibility or automatically hand off every task he or she doesn't like to do. I'm talking about working in a place where your passion and skills intersect. My love for taking people on a journey and my unique gifting to produce events to serve that purpose come together at that intersection. I love serving leaders and creating space for them to meet with their heavenly Father. That's when I'm in my sweet spot.

Don't lose sight of the necessity of operating out of your uniqueness and your God-given set of passions, talents, and gifts. At times we have to do things we don't like, but let's not live lives we don't like.

I'd like you to reread Psalm 139 while you embrace the truth that God made you for a unique purpose. He didn't create just a part of you for a unique purpose. He created all of you for 100 percent of your purpose.

As we move into the process of developing your leadership identity and learning to lead from your truest self, you'll see that it all rests on this truth. In part 2, we will dive deeply into how to find your truest self. Who you are, the you that God created, is the leader your circle of influence wants to see and waits to be led by.

Part 2

Releasing the Life Giver Within You

By now I hope you're encouraged by the truth that you were made for leadership. I'm referring to the person you are—with no reservations—not a version of you that looks like someone else. Just *you.*

I can't emphasize enough how critical this is for your leadership legacy.

It's counterintuitive, but it takes some work to apply all of who you are to your leadership. It requires an intentional investment in yourself that will turn into an investment in others. It might even feel selfish right now, but it's not. It might be the most unselfish thing you can do, because it will benefit the people around you one thousand times over.

Later in this book you will see that I am determined to show you how to lead from a place of authenticity. I like this dictionary definition of *authentic:* "true to one's own personality, spirit, or character; is sincere and authentic with no pretensions."[1]

Authenticity is living and leading in a way that is true to your uniqueness. It feels good and freeing to say that out loud. The goal of finally being true to yourself might well be the reason you picked up this book. Some of us don't even know how to find out who we are.

So much time has passed since we last led from who we are, without allowing our environment to dictate our behavior.

"Authenticity is a collection of choices that we have to make every day," Brené Brown wrote. "It's about the choice to show up and be real. The choice to be honest. The choice to let our true selves be seen."[2]

Letting your true self be seen is a decision you make. You choose to let those around you see you as you are, without any attempt to duplicate another leader's approach or style. You march to your own beat. You act like no one but yourself, and you let the rest follow you.

Your truest self is your authentic self. Leaders who are authentic are also life-giving. It's not an overstatement to say that a life-giving leader must be authentic. It won't work in any other way.

Your leadership legacy starts with who you are, but different streams also flow into it. Life-giving leadership begins with self-awareness and self-acceptance, nonnegotiable hallmarks of authentic leadership. Three additional streams flow into your river of influence. They are self-confidence, humility, and health.

The struggle to become and remain a life-giving leader is worth all the work you will put into it. Ask God for wisdom to give you clarity on each of the five steps. Ask God to show you the power you have to give life to others. And along the way expect to be changed forever.

5

Mirror, Mirror

Life-Giving Leaders Are Self-Aware

My wife, Carrie, is amazing. She's funny. Like really funny. And she's an unbelievable mother. Our boys will probably not understand for a long time just how amazing she is. She is one of the most loyal friends you will ever meet. Whether you reciprocate or not, she's there for you. She's thoughtful and she's beautiful.

I love all these things about my wife. I'm so thankful the Lord gave her to me as my wife. I'm telling you this because I almost missed her.

In college, my ability to relate to women wasn't the strongest. The biggest struggle I faced was, well, just paying attention. My wife and I became great friends after a couple of years' involvement in the Wesley Foundation at the University of Georgia. I could tell you about God's faithfulness there, but that alone could be an entire book!

In my senior year she invited me to be her date at a sorority event. (I like to think it was my dance moves, but apparently there was more at play.) In fact, this happened more than once. We would hang out and eat

Chick-fil-A together. Quite often we would play Ultimate Frisbee with friends. There could be tons of people around, but we would always find each other. We had become amazing friends.

I loved hanging out with her.

Even though she was a great friend and by any measure a real blast, I didn't handle our friendship as well as I could have. I didn't take care of the gift the Lord had given me. I failed to treat our relationship in an honoring way. After dating a couple of times (with my incredible inability to pick up on any cues), we put our relationship on hold. I made it known that I still wanted to be friends, but I had hurt the relationship too much. I had missed the gift who was staring me in the face.

I had been aloof and self-centered. I failed to see what an amazing person had entered my world. Our close friendship was on, then off, then on, then off. Thank goodness the third time was a charm, because I finally figured out the gift I almost missed!

THE IMPORTANCE OF SELF-AWARENESS

Many of us become aware of things quickly, and others take much longer. Ironically, it can be easier to see things clearly when you are an outsider looking in. It can be incredibly difficult for the people involved, who at the time are the ones who most need awareness. It's very similar to the phenomenon of not seeing the forest for the trees. You know it. I know it. But for many of us, it doesn't change things.

Let's bring this down to the life level. Have you ever worked for someone who was completely clueless as to how he or she came across to other people? You know the type: leaders who consider themselves great communicators, but staff members rarely know where the organization is headed, much less what the leader expects of them.

Self-awareness is the foundation for a lifetime of leading well. Knowing yourself unlocks your leadership potential. Conversely, a lack of self-awareness will hurt your leadership potential before it gets off the ground.

Gaining self-awareness can change your leadership forever. It can move you instantly from requiring grace from others—because of your misdirected words and actions—to being a life-giving leader. Leaders who lack awareness of their emotional impact on others will function like a dam in the river of influence, keeping the river from serving its purpose. Poor self-awareness will divert your influence more quickly than you think.

I learned this valuable lesson by accident. I love personality assessments because I enjoy figuring out more about myself. The RightPath assessment has helped me understand that I'm not high in structure (precise, organized, and achieving). Many of us feel we are losing out by not having these gifts or characteristics. For years, the RightPath assessment identified attributes only on one side of the report. It looked like a strengths-and-weaknesses test. You might feel you were strong in a few areas and weak in everything else because, for example, there were no strengths shown in relation to being short on precision, details, and organization. If you scored low in any of the categories, your high categories felt limited.

Thankfully, the RightPath organization didn't leave it that way. Now the assessment provides a more accurate picture of your uniqueness. For instance, you know what the opposite of structured is? Unstructured. That's no surprise, but the attributes of being unstructured are just as amazing as those of being structured. You might lack aptitude in getting every detail nailed down, but you are strong as a generalist, as one who can improvise and use your instincts.

Reading about my strengths was an eye-opener. I had been convinced that I might not have what it takes to be a great leader because I'm not wired to be structured. Want to know what makes my wiring great for doing events? I'm a generalist who's strong at improvising and instinct. If you have done any staging, conference hosting, or major event planning, you know that flexibility and thinking on your feet are strengths. If you insist on sticking to plan A, you'll be frustrated and might even develop an ulcer. Plus the event will suffer as a result.

Like anybody else, I am at my best when I lean into my gift set. When I am working on-site at events, I am flourishing. I love the energy and possibilities at live events. I don't get overwhelmed during the week of an event. I get way more overwhelmed during the months leading up to events because of the detailed planning that's required. When we have issues on-site or are spinning a million plates, that's when it all comes together for me.

You might recall my telling you about some people who, early in my career, said that if I failed, it would be because of my personality. The parts of my personality they didn't like are the exact traits that now make me good at my job. I can lead from a place of authenticity because I have studied myself and become aware of who I am.

You can't lead authentically without knowing your authentic self. This doesn't happen by accident; it requires intentional investment, openness, and a willingness to accept who you truly are. You have to weed through years of tangled, overgrown experiences that have defined you. You and I have so many experiences that have become part of our story, but that doesn't mean they define us accurately. To lead authentically, you first have to prune the lies and nurture the truths. Life-giving leaders go through their past, flower by flower and tree by tree, to discard the lies and enhance the truth. Only then can they lead from a place of life.

EMOTIONAL INTELLIGENCE

In the 1990s Daniel Goleman wrote one of the most important leadership articles in decades. The *Harvard Business Review* published "What Makes a Leader?," which introduced the world to a game-changing concept: emotional intelligence.

Emotional intelligence (EQ) quickly became foundational for leadership. I'll summarize the article, but I strongly encourage you to read it yourself.

Goleman introduced a new paradigm for leaders. My one-sentence summary is this: the best leaders in the world are those who are best at leading people.

It's not that these leaders are the best at managing projects, tasks, or cash flow. Rather, they lead people best. Goleman argued it isn't enough to have a high level of intelligence. More is required. CEOs and other leaders who outperformed their competition tended to be the best at leading people. I have seen this to be true.

Leaders have to execute. I am not arguing that competency and project-management skills are not critical for success. However, Goleman revealed data that supports his theory that the best leaders lead people best. The soft skills possessed by the best leaders proved to be the difference makers in their ability to lead.

I believe most life-giving leaders understand the emotional effect, good and bad, their decisions and their words have on the people around them. That's emotional intelligence at its core. One of the most prominent attributes identified by Goleman is self-awareness. I have seen it function as the most foundational attribute to building teams, just as love is foundational to raising children. Self-awareness is the starting point to building your leadership legacy.

Let's do a quick exercise related to this attribute. Think about someone you know (friend, family member, coworker, boss) who lacks self-awareness. In what area does this person need greater awareness? What is his or her blind spot?

Now, think about how this person's lack of self-awareness affects you.

How frustrating is it that this person remains unaware of how she or he interacts with others?

Now we'll bring things even closer to home. What is it like to be on the other side of me? My friend Jeff Henderson asked that question in a staff meeting. What are you like to others? Are you aware of your posture and attitude? Are you aware that you sometimes (or often) fail to pick up on social cues?

You are always the common denominator in every situation you are in.

I have seen people who bounce from job to job or church to church because someone in the company or organization doesn't live up to their expectations. I know people who have become almost unhirable because it was always the boss's fault they didn't succeed at their previous place of employment. Or they leave a company after they failed to get a promotion, and the same things happen again in their next job. After a series of such experiences, I would expect these people to ask about the common denominator. In every instance, the one person always present was the dissatisfied person.

At times leaders number among the perpetually dissatisfied. But leaders who choose to deflect and look at other people's issues instead of their own will not be life-giving. They will have a short-lived influence at best. Life-giving leaders take responsibility and are then normally given more responsibility. When you own it, you get more of it.

Life-giving leaders understand their impact on other people. This understanding allows them to choose a direction of life flow. When they understand their uniqueness, they understand how they uniquely affect the people around them.

Leaders are learners. And the best leaders work hard to learn about themselves. I would argue that life-giving leaders are the best learners because they are the best students of themselves, their leadership, and their impact.

Your leadership legacy will grow when it begins with awareness. It is the foundation. How will you know how to lead from your truest self if you don't know who that person is?

Look in the Mirror

The first time I took an intentional step into self-awareness followed a 360 evaluation. My coach and longtime friend Fran LaMattina helped administer it. A 360 is an evaluation that gives people in your life (bosses, peers, direct reports, friends, and family) an opportunity to be honest with you about your leadership.

As you've already guessed, it's really hard. Even when the response to you is generally positive, it's hard. Because of the vulnerability required, the effectiveness of the 360 calls for an intentional group of raters who are mature enough to handle an anonymous assessment of you. It also requires an expert to administer it. (This is critical; otherwise the 360 can be damaging.)

In my first 360, the raters gave me high scores on leadership, relationships, and more. Even Fran told me it was a really good reflection and that I should be proud of it.

As valuable as candid outside input can be, it seldom matches our self-assessment. Our natural tendency is to congratulate ourselves on any positive feedback we receive, assuming it captures our overall style. Or we focus on the areas that need work and then try to fight off despair. I am off-the-charts positive, but when the 360 results came back, my eyes rushed to the negative comments.

Two areas were said to need additional work. One was time management; the other was listening. I wasn't surprised that time management was singled out. I'm good at arriving on time, but I don't manage my time and schedule well.

The mention of listening, however, threw me for a loop. Bear in mind it was my team that did the rankings of strengths and weaknesses.

I mean, come on. I'm relational! Doesn't that automatically make me a good listener? Of course not. I was not good at controlling my body language when I checked out, got bored, or had no interest in the subject at hand. When my body language announced I didn't care about a discussion topic or agenda item, my team felt as though I wasn't listening.

You might see yourself in some of the results of my 360. When your team perceives that you're not listening because your vibe indicates as such, it means you're not. This is worth your attention.

Feedback is valuable when it's done right. You choose when you get feedback and how it's done. When the process is one of integrity and guided by a specialist in the field, you should take it seriously. You can be offended by the outcome and ignore it, or you can acknowledge it, dig in, and search for the answer to what is happening. Life-giving leaders learn from legitimate input because they want to grow in self-awareness.

My staff gave feedback because they wanted me to grow as a leader. As much as it hurt, the process made me a better life-giving leader.

My longtime friend and production director would say, "Looks as if you're done with this conversation!" I had given him permission to call me out. Those moments helped me see the times when I wasn't listening. Did I suddenly become the world's best listener? No! But it's helpful to talk to your team about the awareness you have regarding your needed areas of growth. That way, they can help you see the blind spots in the day-to-day workflow.

I'm not sure I will ever become a great listener, but I will work to become better at it. I want to invite you to pause here for a second. When was the last time you allowed people who want what's best for you to be honest about your strengths and weaknesses? Some of you need to schedule a time for this. Create a plan to figure out the areas you need to pay more attention to. What if we all agree to do something about this in the next thirty days? Even if you've done this before, it might be time to check back in. You know and I know it's not easy, but it's important.

AWARENESS AREAS

Let's make this concept practical. There are many areas in which accurate awareness can make or break our leadership. I want to look at seven areas of awareness that each of us needs to consider to ensure our foundation is solid. Hundreds of areas affect us, but these seven come up over and over again.

1. Emotional Awareness

Think of someone you know who has no idea how to deal with his or her emotions. How does that affect the person's leadership? It would be difficult for me to think of a great leader who doesn't have at least some awareness of his or her emotions and emotional well-being.

Raising two boys who like to mess with each other has taught me a valuable lesson. It's important to learn what anger looks and feels like, and it's just as important to learn how to control your anger. You and I are handed a million opportunities every week to get angry, and we often handle our anger poorly. Some leaders have put great coping mechanisms in place to handle adversity, anger, frustration, and related emotions. But many have not. These emotions will come out at some point. Either you pick how they are expressed or they will express themselves without your managing them. Usually when you let your emotions choose, you lose. What if exercise, fishing, sewing, reading, or something similar became your way of blowing off steam instead of losing it by raising your voice, getting red in the face, and saying things that are damaging to other people?

Some leaders at the top of organizational charts never learn how to successfully deal with strong negative emotions. You will slow the flow of life if you don't learn to properly control emotions. Organizations tend to take on the leader's personality, good or bad. With that in view, it's easy to see how quickly organizations can lose control of emotions when the leader does. Hence, the importance of this becoming a self-initiated exercise and a focus of self-awareness.

2. Awareness of History

Leaders have to be aware of their past and its effects on them. I'm often amazed at the lack of attention leaders give their history.

When I was a freshman in college, my family went through a pretty tough financial stretch. Things got even tougher after some additional financial developments. When you go through that in your formative years, it makes a lasting emotional impression on you. Even today, financial insecurity is very emotional to me. It makes me nervous and frustrated. I have spent the past twenty-plus years processing that part of my past to understand how it colors the way I react to new situations.

One time a company I was part of had a challenging financial situation arise. It was amazing to see how each executive handled the problem. Some were emotional (like me) and some were convinced it was no big deal. I'm sure my emotional reaction to the situation bothered some of my colleagues. But I have found that awareness leads to learning.

If we fail to study how our history affects the way we act and respond, we won't be prepared for circumstances outside our control. Go to counseling if necessary. Wrestle with your past and figure out why you respond in certain ways. Dig in to your family and understand how they think and respond. It will be hard, but you'll be better for it.

3. Awareness of Relational Tendencies and Keys

A great reason to use assessments (such as RightPath, StrengthsFinder, and the Enneagram) is to gain important insight into your relational tendencies. I want to learn more and more about my wiring so I can better understand how I relate to work and people.

For about ten years I worked at two satellite churches of North Point Ministries. This was an awesome time in my life. I served as the service programming director at our Browns Bridge campus, which was the second of the two churches. During that time I had two amazing bosses. They were great leaders whom I loved working for, and I was spared any frequent turnover in leaders. (I had two bosses in seven years.) We all need to be thankful when we have some consistency in this regard.

It took me about two years to learn the values of Lane Jones, my first boss there. We had to learn each other. I became aware of how he thought and what tended to make him anxious about our services. After about five years, Lane headed back to another of the church campuses and a new boss came flying in. Clay Scroggins became a very close friend and turned into a fantastic leader.

Based on some of the things I had learned about Lane, I asked Clay in the first couple of weeks what he valued most in the service. That simple question saved me months of trying to learn him. I still had to be a good student of my leader. But when you can learn some of their key values up front, it helps get the party going and it helps things progress more smoothly.

Learning about yourself through assessments, coaching, and evaluations lets you give new people relational keys and understandings up front. From the beginning, my team members learned that I need space to process out loud. My team has to help me turn my talk into action. They need to understand I am crazy optimistic, and it can lead to me saying yes to more than we can handle or need to do.

You see, with three sentences I made you aware of what it is like to work with me. How many of you would love to know that about your current boss? It is a gift to those around you to have such understandings. Great awareness starts with studying yourself and how you naturally relate to others.

4. Awareness of Confrontation Style

One of the most important gifts that comes with learning your wiring is understanding how each new revelation spills over into other areas. For example, increasing your emotional awareness helps you understand how you deal with conflict. When you understand how you naturally relate to other people and identify your emotional hot buttons, you will understand how you respond best to conflict. Hardly anyone likes conflict. Those who do need to learn how to tone it down, and those who don't need to learn how to lean into it a little more.

As believers, we have given up the right to not deal with conflict. We have to keep short accounts. Not just because Jesus tells us to but because it is a much better life when we do. Bitterness, tension, and conflict will crush us. Great leaders understand they have to cut conflict off quickly and at the source.

Becoming aware of your confrontation style will allow you to have the least collateral damage, because you will be striving to understand the other person's wiring as well. This is quite simple. Choose a personality assessment (pick from one of those mentioned earlier) and have your organization or team take it together. Then look through the assessment and determine the way each person best receives hard conversations. Being able to approach each person well and in ways that honor the individual will go far in defusing the conflict at hand. If you fail to understand the other leader's wiring—with or without understanding your own confrontation style—a relational bomb can be set off, causing damage that might never be repairable.

Again, you can be right on a point. But if you approach the issue in the wrong way, you are no longer right. Confrontation awareness could potentially be the upgrade you need to move to the next level in your leadership.

5. Awareness of Your Posture

This one should be self-explanatory. But like most self-evident things, it's often the furthest thing from a leader's mind. One's posture encompasses everything from body language to punctuality. It's how you come across to people without saying anything.

I feel so strongly about posture that if a staff member fails to grow in life-giving posture, it's an indication that it may be time for that person to move on to new opportunities elsewhere. If you roll your eyes or have trouble controlling your sighs and overall body language, you can't be a life-giving leader. It is important that your posture matches your words. If you say you're all in, but your posture tells me something else, that's a problem. When leaders choose good posture, team members pay attention to them. When leaders have a positive posture, they usually gain favor with those around them. Smiling, active listening, sitting up straight, and paying attention are examples of posture that make others notice you.

Ask around and find out how you're perceived. Figure out when people can tell you're not listening. Understand how you come across when you're bored or frustrated. Leaders need to regulate their body language and posture.

6. Awareness of Your Tone

Tone might be one of the most difficult and most critical of the seven areas of awareness. Tone refers to how you say things, not what you say. Your tone can make something more clear or crush communication. An ever-present example of this dynamic is social media and other instant-communication technology. It is killing our ability to experience proper tone.

Email, text messages, Twitter, Snapchat, Slack, WhatsApp, instant messaging, and other communication tools all omit one thing: context. You can't hear tone in words appearing on a screen. You can't see the smile on the other person's face as he or she gently jokes with you. And emojis only mask a person's tone, because you can throw a winking emoji onto the end of a passive-aggressive text and it will communicate an inaccurate, misleading tone. We have lost the art of dialogue and relationship building.

Of course, text and email are time-saving technologies. They make picking up the phone or setting up a meeting seem like an irresponsible waste of time. However, there is potential for inflicting great damage every time you handle a digital communication poorly. Without being able to convey tone, it is difficult to monitor or predict how your words will be received.

Life-giving leaders aim for positive and life-giving tone. Even when you have to have difficult in-person discussions (on the phone or face to face), it removes the guesswork when it comes to tone. The other person is not forced to guess your emotional state. And in situations when you must rely on email, ask someone unrelated to the situation to read your message before you send it. You won't be able to do that for all communication, but every time you take this step, you will protect yourself from unwanted miscommunication.

One more thing: if you learn tone early in your career, it will grow your influence like wildfire. When leaders around me handle questions, conflict, brainstorming, or even joking with good tone, it tells me a ton about their awareness and their heart.

7. Awareness of Your Motivation

What makes you tick? What drives you to achieve? How do you push for success? What deters you from being your best?

Questions such as these are important to help us become aware of how we are motivated. Motivation also ranks among the five components of emotional intelligence. What motivates you is just as important to your awareness as the other areas we've talked about. When you learn what drives you and become aware of how that motivation shows up in your day-to-day leadership, you will begin to handle it with maturity.

For example, if you are a driven individual who wants to achieve something at all costs, you will very likely crush some people along the way. If you ask those who are highly driven to achieve, I would bet they will talk about having accomplished a difficult task but leaving a number of bodies in their wake—that is, if they are aware of how their motivation affects their relationships.

Maybe you're naturally motivated by empowering other people. Learning to see how that motivation can push you in other areas (communication, details, organization, and so on) will potentially make you even better at empowering others by serving them in different ways.

Don't overlook the importance of this aspect of self-awareness. If you are highly motivated by achievement for achievement's sake, you have to understand how that affects other people. I'm not naturally motivated to just achieve, but helping others achieve motivates me. That's my motivation and it drives me. Beyond that awareness, I needed to change my leadership approach to motivate myself and others to achieve at different times and in different ways.

Your Legacy Starts with Awareness

We have scratched the surface of the awareness we need to have as leaders. The river of leadership legacy starts here and grows daily when you work on self-awareness.

The bad news? If you don't create a foundational understanding of who you are, you will probably have a river that grows sluggish and strays outside its intended channel. Such rivers never increase in the ability to give life to more organisms. Most of the rivers that slow down become swamps or get dammed up. Unaware leaders are their own worst enemies.

Imagine working for a leader who has great self-awareness. Imagine that person developing an accurate understanding of how he or she best handles conflict. How body language can create emotional distress or release tension. Imagine your leader being intent on discovering how the past plays into the present.

Imagine you being that leader. Can you see how being this kind of leader will almost instantly add more influence to your flow? Can you see how this is the beginning of a life-giving leader's legacy?

You can do this. Performing this internal examination and study will set you on a course in which life flows from you and is not required for you from others.

Awareness opens the way for life to flow. And then influence grows.

6

Schoolyard Sports

Life-Giving Leaders Are Self-Accepting

When I was in seminary, I, along with several other seminary students, worked one month in the summer investing in fifty high schoolers. One student who stood out was a young man born with no hands. He had use of his arms to his wrists but no hands.

He was one of the most positive and energetic people I've ever met. There was nothing he couldn't do. We spent a week in the Adirondack Mountains and a week in Guatemala. He joined the other students in swinging through the trees on the high-ropes courses. He was always smiling and cracking jokes.

I found out that he had chosen early in life to accept who he was and the circumstances given to him. So many leaders have issues that pale in comparison, and yet they have never accepted who they are.

Buckle up, leaders. We're going on a ride. Honestly, this might be the most difficult chapter in the book to work through. It will probably require the deepest dive.

While this step is the most difficult, it is also the most powerful. In my opinion, this is where most leaders stop developing because it requires hard work and long looks in the mirror. Social media and today's culture make these things difficult, and our childhood dynamics make them challenging.

Self-acceptance is very likely one of the hardest leadership obstacles you'll ever tackle.

I'll use kickball as an example. As Ricky Bobby says in the movie *Talladega Nights,* "If you ain't first, you're last."[1] Isn't that the way it felt during school recess as team captains were picking players? The process made many of us tremble with anxiety. And while elementary and middle school are now distant memories, we hold on to an insatiable desire to feel accepted and wanted. We all experience the joy that comes with acceptance, and we all suffer the hurt of rejection. I bet every one of us has felt these things. And unfortunately many of us allow a desire for acceptance and the avoidance of rejection to drive us.

People watch *60 Minutes* or *20/20* partly because these shows often air stories of overcomers. We are drawn to stories about people who have not let their circumstances define them. We admire leaders who use the hard things to pave the way for better things to come. They turn tragedy into triumph.

It's not easy to accept ourselves completely, but it's necessary. If we don't learn to accept who we are, we'll never be the leaders God made us to be. And this won't be something we'll work on for a week and then never have to think about again. Accepting ourselves is a lifetime pursuit. We all have seen personal insecurity show up just when we thought we had overcome it. It's as if our struggle to embrace who we really are simply covered up our insecurity for a moment before it popped up again.

Don't be surprised if you take a step forward and then life happens and you take two steps backward. Out of all five steps to life-giving leadership, this is the one where most leaders get stuck. Some of us will need to seek professional help to overcome the emotions attached to accepting who we are.

We know that God wants to give us a breakthrough in this area. It is His design, after all, that we criticize when we find ourselves lacking. A life-giving leader embraces his or her self as the unerring design of God, meant as a unique gift to each of us. The flow of life from your leadership will continue to be limited until you reach a place of acceptance.

FOUR KEYS TO SELF-ACCEPTANCE

FOMO, short for "fear of missing out," captures the feeling of wishing you could do something you know others are involved in. It also applies to wanting to be where your friends are. A deeper, valid emotion is attached to FOMO. It's more than just wishing to have the same experience or adventure your friends are enjoying. It is, in fact, the same emotion we felt when we weren't picked for kickball. It's the feeling of not being accepted.

That feeling puts knots in our stomachs. We feel left out and left behind. We feel unwanted, and we assume the rejection is based on who we are. The feeling goes to our core. What we often overlook is that we are making life harder for ourselves. We create unnecessary burdens for ourselves when we spend our lives wishing we were somebody else and wanting what other people have.

Why weigh ourselves down with feelings of having less than others, of experiencing less than others, and of being less than others? Let the truth of our design free us of unnecessary baggage. Welcome the truth of God about who we are (you might want to reread Psalm 139). God's truth is this: *we have been made uniquely for a unique purpose.*

I tell young leaders the more quickly you can take pride in your uniqueness, the sooner you will become a great leader. As we learned in chapter 4, our heavenly Father knitted us together in our mothers' wombs. And we know God never makes mistakes. There's no question that our childhoods, our relationships, and our decisions have at times damaged our understanding of who we are. But our wiring—our personality, strengths, aptitudes, motivations—is a gift from the Lord. Just as someone else's wiring is a gift to him or her.

Following are the four action steps to accepting your uniqueness. Let God use these keys to unlock and upgrade your leadership and help you accept who you are.

1. Learn to Love Yourself

It's been said that happiness can exist only in acceptance. I will go one step further and say that until you accept the gift of your uniqueness, you cannot enjoy it.

A crazy cultural swing in the Christian community currently de-emphasizes receiving. Many people would call it false humility, but I think we just have a hard time receiving gifts. Something has happened that makes us feel unworthy, so we have trouble receiving anything we feel we don't deserve or that we haven't paid for. I know I have a hard time with it.

Have you ever been given a gift that you knew cost the giver dearly? Let's flip that. Have you ever given a gift to someone who was reluctant to accept it? How did you feel? In some Christian circles, it's almost a game for people to sacrifice by only giving and never receiving. What we need to accept is that receiving allows God to use and grow the giver.

If we never learn how to receive, we will never learn how to accept. If we don't accept who God made us to be, we will never receive the true gift He has given us. For many people, loving yourself for who you are is incredibly difficult. Many of us have simple hurdles to get over and can work through things on our own. We need to work through areas of shame, frustration, and regret because of past decisions, family situations, or leadership missteps and failures. If you feel as if your past is crushing your ability to do this, however, find a counselor or therapist to help you move forward. Or you might begin by talking with a trusted friend. Either way, accepting yourself will require time spent excavating your past so you can move into your future.

Being okay with who you are does not mean you don't have flaws; it means you have grown to like how you live, work, and play. You accept how you process decisions, what makes you laugh and cry, and the way you create art, dance, or build furniture.

You also need to accept your spiritual style. Gary Thomas's book *Sacred Pathways* is one of my favorites on a person's unique worship style and connection with God. Learning and embracing your wiring to relate to people and the Lord will give you a freedom of expression as nothing before. For me, being outside is the place I connect the most. I feel the most "me" when I'm outdoors. Where do you feel most alive? Identify that, then look for ways to incorporate that environment more into your daily life.

I began early to search for ways to accept myself. Even in high school, I was okay with me for the most part. I recently completed an exercise in which I looked back at the highs and lows of my life. I recall that even in middle school I was thankful that God gave me the gift of being good with who I was. I still struggled with insecurity, fear, and everything that came with peer pressure and the need to fit in. But because I was okay with me and proud of my uniqueness, I was able to stay true to myself through the formative years. Self-acceptance helped me avoid places and people I felt might discredit my decisions and convictions. I never really felt as if I had to adjust my personality to be like the cool kids or the smart kids or any other group in school.

Throughout my life, I have seen that the most attractive leaders to work for have tapped into their own uniqueness, which has allowed them to stay steady.

2. Stop Chasing Other People's Uniqueness

Social media has become not just a daily or weekly indulgence but an hourly (or even more frequent than hourly) distraction from the everyday routine of life. In saying this, I am not labeling social media as the enemy. I love it.

However, it can become a massive distraction from our work, our goals, our calling, and our ability to be okay with ourselves. It also serves to medicate away the realities and feelings we want to ignore. We all know that the life portrayed on social media is a glorified version of an ordinary life. But even though on some level we know that to be true, I still know some people who compare every part of their lives with the travel, adventures, success, beauty, and romance they see posted all over social media.

Subjecting ourselves to the purported perfection of other people is not a recommended step toward self-acceptance. Neither is it recommended to study the claims made by self-proclaimed perfect leaders who enjoy mentioning growth in all the metrics that are said to matter. Social media virtually glows with updates on the leader's new book, new expanded ministry, new satellite campus, new capital campaign, and dramatic rise in attendance, membership, volunteers, and mission trips. You and I, if we indulge in scrolling through the news feed, see it all displayed for us to covet.

You and I know we should never compare ourselves with anyone else. You are the *only* you alive. God made sure of that. But come on. We're curious about other leaders, other work environments, other measures of effectiveness. It's almost impossible to avoid looking in on how other leaders are doing, and when we do, it's almost impossible not to be drawn into wanting what they have.

Life-giving leaders embrace who they are and avoid chasing other people's uniqueness. I've said this a few different ways, and I don't apologize for that. It's important enough that we need to hear it more than once. When you spend your life chasing something that isn't attainable because it doesn't come from your uniqueness, you will be sorely disappointed. And why should any of us go out of our way to create more disappointment for ourselves?

Tom Brady, quarterback of the New England Patriots, is one of the greatest players at that position the NFL has ever seen. Since 2000, Brady has become an icon of American football. Either you love Brady or you don't, but you can't deny the team's impressive winning record with him at the helm.

As a lifelong Atlanta Falcons fan, I don't like Brady. His team beat my team in Super Bowl LI. It's not as if the Patriots were hard up for another Super Bowl win. At the time they met the Falcons in the championship game, they had already won four Super Bowls. Did they really need a fifth?

And dominance on the football field is not all. Tom Brady looks like a *GQ* model. If you indulge in the celebrity media frenzy, you can't help but see photo after photo of him with his supermodel wife. I'm not kidding about any of this. You might think the best NFL quarterback in history is a lumpy-looking Grabowski with a flattened nose, multiple visible scars, a slight limp, and a beer gut. You'd think wrong. In 2005 this poster boy for good looks won his third Super Bowl. He was just twenty-seven years old. So now we can add that Brady was already super successful (beyond belief) *at a young age.* Can you stand any more of this?

Steve Kroft from *60 Minutes* interviewed Brady. Two insights from their conversation are breathtaking. The first is Brady's understanding of what he can and cannot do. Even at his skill level in his chosen profession, top players still want to do things other players can do. (It's not just you and me.) But not Brady. He has excelled in a very, very difficult, competitive field while doing one thing. He plays like Tom Brady and no one else.

Listen to what he said on this point:

> With those strengths and weaknesses, you do play to your
> strengths and you try to improve your weaknesses. . . . A lot of
> guys are very mobile, and they can do a lot of great things when
> the plays break down and when they're moving out of the pocket.
> It's fun to watch. I mean, I see [former NFL quarterback] Michael

Vick do that, and I say, "Geez, that guy is terrific, and I can't do that. It's impossible, no matter how hard I try only bad things are going to happen." So, why try it? I mean, the best thing for me is to know what the defense is going to do and to drop back and throw the ball to the guy who's most open and let him run. And if I don't do that, then we won't win. And that's not fun.[2]

Don't miss the wisdom here. The best thing Brady can do is play *his* game. If he tries to be someone else, the Patriots are likely to lose, and that's not fun. I love his honesty and understanding. We can all learn from this celebrated NFL quarterback about understanding our own unique role.

In the interview, Brady went on to make one of the most profound statements I've heard from a professional athlete.

Why do I have three Super Bowl rings [at the time of the interview], and still think there's something greater out there for me? I mean, maybe a lot of people would say, "Hey man, this is what is." I reached my goal, my dream, my life. Me, I think: God, it's gotta be more than this. I mean this can't be what it's all cracked up to be. I mean I've done it. I'm 27. And what else is there for me?[3]

His entire life has been built around chasing Super Bowl rings. He will finish with more rings than the vast majority of players who have played in the history of the NFL. And yet that pursuit does not solve the search for worth and life. When you chase something that gives temporary relief or celebration, you wake up the next day and ask, "What's next?"

When you chase other people's uniqueness, you will never be satisfied. Only the pursuit of your relationship with God can ultimately fulfill you.

Imagine if there were a generation of leaders who chose to trust that what God says is true. First, they would believe that how He made them is good. Second, it would transform their lives, their work, and their leadership. Imagine a workforce filled with leaders who are pursuing improvement instead of working hard to be people they are not. Imagine a church filled with leaders who have embraced their God-given uniqueness and who are leaning into their gifts to line up with God's plan for their lives.

3. Seek Freedom from Wrong Expectations

One of the most difficult aspects of leadership is maintaining proper expectations of others. Even more, it's critical to focus on appropriate expectations for yourself.

Isn't it true that many of the times you've experienced miscommunication with a leader, it was because of an unclear or incorrect expectation? This situation is common. How many times have you been frustrated with a staff member who didn't do what you expected, and then you realized, *How would they know what I expect if I haven't told them?*

I often remind my leadership team that when individuals aren't performing up to standards, we have to ask the following: Are they where we've led them? Have we fully communicated expectations and clarified what success looks like? People can't hit the right target if they don't know which target to aim for.

It's the same with your own leadership. When you allow the expectations of other people to define you, you will probably lose. But when you refuse to hold up the abilities of other leaders as the standard, you free yourself to succeed as the leader you are called to be.

None of us can live up to the expectations of other people. The main reason for this is that such expectations are based on the people's perceptions of us and the situation, which almost never fit the facts. So you need to have clear conversations with the people around you (those who lead you and the people on your team). Understand their expectations, make clear who you are as a person and as a leader, and come to a shared understanding as that pertains to expectations.

Many times I have set (or reset) expectations by explaining why I have delegated certain responsibilities to specific leaders. At the same time, having clear conversations about areas you are working to grow in, either to your boss or to those who report to you, allows everyone's expectations to be clarified.

4. Recognize That Integrity Lies at the Root of Acceptance

Once you've accepted yourself, you then have to pursue the values, beliefs, convictions, and attributes that match who you are. Integrity is one of the greatest values a leader can possess. Being a man or woman of your word is priceless and results from a constant fight to be who God made you to be. A person who is known for honesty is one who owns his or her mistakes. This is the leader who is respected by the team.

I've given a lot of thought to the importance of integrity in a leader, and I've concluded that consistency is a primary reason integrity is so attractive.

When you talk about the integrity of a wall or a bridge, you are referring to its consistency. You can expect a load-bearing wall to keep the ceiling and the floor above it from falling on your head. You can expect a bridge to be constructed in such a way that you will be able to safely cross a river. As it pertains to leaders, integrity means other people can trust the leader to do what he or she is made to do. Which brings us back to self-acceptance. To be filled with integrity, you have to accept your uniqueness.

Leaders were made to lead and bring life to the people they lead. If you don't know who you are, your people won't know whom to expect. Which leader showed up today? If your team has to monitor your moods before they ask a question or raise an issue, they will lose confidence in you as a leader.

I'm not saying you can't have bad days, but let those days be the exception to the rule. Make sure your team members stay on their toes and remain confident in your leadership instead of on their heels and always wondering which boss will be at work today. When you lead from a place of consistency and integrity, your self-acceptance will be strengthened and others will be challenged to do the same.

I can't tell you how many leaders I know who are desperate for a leader to be consistent and for a leader who is worth following. A leader who doesn't pretend to be someone else is a leader who is consistent. These are hallmarks of life-giving leaders.

WHAT DO WE DO?

This is life-giving advice, and it's hard work. That's why so many leaders never move past this step in the process. The number of leaders who could move from good to unbelievable leadership is limited because of the difficulty of these steps. Each step requires perseverance.

Acceptance requires trust that what God says is true. Trust that God did not make a mistake with you. Trust that you have been given a gift and you need to receive it.

I'm not trying to simplify this. I can't, because it is loaded with complications. However, to become a life-giving leader, you have to first be proud of the life you lead, and that centers on your wiring. Here are a few ideas for the next steps in accepting your leadership:

- Ask the Lord for peace. Ask for wisdom about how this works within the calling He has for you.
- Invite a few close friends to help you see the unique leadership gifts God has given you.
- Choose one unique attribute of your leadership that you decide to accept and take pride in, and then lean into that strength this week.

Pick one of these three ideas. Today, plan a time to focus on accepting yourself. When you work to accept yourself, you will be amazed at how quickly and naturally life begins to flow to others in ways you would've never imagined.

7

It's Like Riding a Bike

Life-Giving Leaders Are Self-Confident

In 2014, after a retirement filled with drama, partying, and boredom, Michael Phelps decided to swim again. The most decorated Olympian of all time announced he would compete at the Olympics in Rio de Janeiro.

At that time, he had twenty-two medals—eighteen of them gold. That's not a typo. He had won eighteen *gold* medals. What could he possibly have left to prove? What more could he show the world that he hadn't already abundantly demonstrated? He had accomplished more than anyone else, and he most likely was financially stable.

In an interview, Phelps talked about needing structure and consistency in his life. Prior to the start of the Rio games, his close friends, including his coach, talked about the fun they were having at the pool. They were relaxing instead of being intense all the time. It seemed to many people who were close to Phelps that getting back to swimming let him live the life he knew best.

I believe the desire for his old life contributed to his return, but I think something deep down also pushed Phelps. I would argue that he was led by his confidence. He knew he could do it.

This is not an isolated incident. At this level, competing in any sport requires immense confidence. Even a far less physically daunting sport such as golf demands vast amounts of confidence. When you have confidence in your swing, you see the difference in your drives and your score.

This helps explain why so many follow the PGA Tour. Watching the pros hit shots we all wish we could hit is mesmerizing. They have made those shots so many times in practice that their confidence comes through during competition.

But not for every golfer and not in every competition. Even on the PGA Tour we see players unravel on the course because they lose confidence in their swing. One wrong thought and down they go.

But something beautiful happens when a golfer allows his or her inner confidence to take over. Watching Tiger Woods in his prime was special. His confidence intimidated other golfers. Only a few players loved going head-to-head with him. He was just that good. (We will talk later about the difference between arrogance and confidence. There's a good reason I started with confidence.)

Over the past few years, Tiger Woods has lost the confidence that served him so well. There's no question that his off-the-course life contributed to some of this insecurity with his game, but the main problem has been physical. When he was at the top, confidence flowed through every aspect of his game. He knew he could hit the shot, not only because of his incredible swing, but also because he trusted his body to work as he needed it to. Ever since his first round of back surgeries, however, he hasn't been the same. The pain of injuries can crush your game and then you stop trusting your body's ability to do what your mind tells it to do.

Life-giving leadership requires you to lead confidently from your truest self and to trust that you have what it takes to make it happen, to finish the project, to develop the staff, to make wise financial plans and decisions, and to bring life to the people you lead. When you lead confidently, people have a sense that you are going somewhere and they want to go with you.

Is there a chance that confidence will turn to arrogance? Yes. Is there a chance that when you ride a bike you might get hurt? Yes. You don't stop riding because of that, and you don't stop fighting to be a confident leader because you're afraid of becoming arrogant. To help guard against arrogance you need to have people in place to help you keep your attitude in check. Trusted colleagues and friends can keep you focused on the main thing. They will keep up with what you're doing and how you're doing it, and they will say something if you are getting close to the line.

One of the greatest coaches in NFL history was Vince Lombardi. The Super Bowl trophy is named in honor of this legendary Green Bay Packers coach. I love what Lombardi said about confidence: "Confidence is contagious. So is lack of confidence."[1]

Did that sting a little? Hit a little too close to home? It does for me. It's hard to admit and yet it's entirely true. Have you ever had to work with or for someone who lacked confidence? It can be painful to watch. It is even more painful to have to work around.

On the other hand, a leader who exudes confidence can turn a team or situation around in the right way. Displaying a lack of confidence also has an impact, but not the impact anyone wants. Insecurity, which is the opposite of confidence, will never bring life to others; it will cause only fear and anxiety.

CONFIDENCE IN CALLING

Have you ever been around people who were extremely confident in what they were made to do? Were you fired up by being around them? Did they make you feel better or worse about the confidence you have in your calling? When I'm around a leader like that, I want what he or she has. Not in a coveting way but in a powerful way. It makes me want to dig in more deeply to understand my own purpose and plan.

This is a very personal chapter for me. Developing and maintaining self-confidence is what I've been dealing with most consistently over the past four years. I continue to work on other areas as well, but I feel as though self-confidence requires the most focus and attention.

I haven't always been confident in my calling. I struggled with this when I took over as executive director of Catalyst in 2013. It was weird. I was confident in my ability to lead the organization and the people, but I still questioned why God would pick me to carry it out. For the first year and a half, I made jokes about God's sense of humor by His putting me in this role. Every time I would introduce myself from the stage, I would tell the audience about my role. Then I'd say, "But I'm not sure what God was thinking when He picked me for this!"

Humor has always been a defense mechanism for me. Anytime I get uncomfortable, it's revealed through my self-deprecating jokes. For eighteen months or so I operated in that mind-set. I led like a pro behind the scenes but publicly joked about God's calling.

That's when a few friends started pushing me on this issue. God had already begun working on my heart. When I made the joke in the presence of a few close friends, a couple of them gave me "the look." You know, the one that says, *Are you kidding me right now?* When I saw their reaction, my heart sank. They pushed me pretty far on the subject, and I realized that when I made jokes about God's plan and calling, I was dishonoring God. In a sense I was making light of God's sovereignty and purposes for my life and leadership.

Here's the crazy thing, though. For more than ten years, I had been calling out those unique plans and designs in the lives of other leaders, and yet I couldn't recognize God's working in my own life! The process of coming to this realization took time and a lot of work. That explains why most leaders never fully grasp this step. Insecurity holds them in its grip. Failure can keep leaders from entering the game. The fear of failure can paralyze leaders, which tends to stop progress and scare off staff members.

So how do we overcome these obstacles to become more confident? We focus on practice and prayer.

First, you will never become confident without practicing the art of trusting yourself. Trusting your God-given abilities and intellect, and trusting your experience and learning, will help you make wise decisions.

Second, and I'm not trying to overspiritualize this, we have to work through these areas in prayer. The fruit of the Spirit, described in Galatians 5:22–23, overflows from your heart and soul as you lead others. Confidence in your calling flows out of your heart's condition. The Lord gives you confidence. Thank Him and remember His faithfulness to you. This will build your faith.

Leaders, it's time we get better! I had to do better. Then God gave me a beautiful New Testament picture that solidified my ability to lean in and become confident in His calling in my life. Calling is so close to who we are and how we operate that Paul mentioned it when he began a letter to the Christians in Corinth. "Paul, *called by the will of God* to be an apostle of Christ Jesus" (1 Corinthians 1:1). Eugene Peterson translates it this way in *The Message:* "I, Paul, have been called and sent by Jesus, the Messiah."

Paul talked about God's plan and calling in his life as something that was given to him. He accepted it and then he proclaimed it. He lived it and preached it. He didn't always live it out perfectly, but that didn't change his belief that God chose him for the job.

Do you see the power of this? Some of you are reading this book for this section alone. You can and should be confident in your calling. Does that statement sound arrogant? No, it sounds like an affirmation made by a leader who trusts God and who accepts that God has placed him where he can best be aligned with his Father. God's will can be accomplished through leaders who embrace this heavenly confidence.

Life-giving leaders lead from a place of confidence. When you show confidence in your own calling, your team will find it easier to have confidence in you. They will trust you. Moreover, they will trust your confidence in them and their calling. When you push them to be confident, it will make sense to them.

It's funny now to look back and see the moments when God began building confidence in me and in my leadership. One of my unique traits is that I'm not intimidated when I'm around other leaders. I don't get starstruck even when I'm around leaders I highly admire. (Well, I got a little starstruck when I met Tony Hawk. His name is near the top of the list of the cool people I've met.) Almost always I can see other leaders for who they are: men and women called by God. I believe in respecting and honoring the leaders who went ahead of us and whose wisdom we continue to learn from. I just don't revere them, which would make it hard for me to lead them if I needed to.

About eight years ago I was working on a church staff and leading the staff in an exercise. After the exercise, a close friend said, "Do you realize how unique your leadership is? You were leading leaders and doing it with such confidence and a lack of intimidation."

Leaders big and small are still humans. We all like to be led with respect and grace, but also with direction and confidence. If you're not confident when you lead others, it will be obvious and will take longer for people to decide to follow you.

THE KEYS TO CONFIDENCE

What if you're not a naturally confident person but you're called to leadership? What will you do when your calling places you in a situation you feel singularly unqualified for?

Conversely, what about leaders whose confidence has turned to arrogance? Is having too much confidence a danger? Are arrogant leaders guilty of doing the right thing in being confident but taking it too far?

In this book I'm presenting the ideal for leaders. This gives us all something to aim for as we develop as leaders. A leader operating at his or her full potential will change the game more than a leader who is bogged down in one of the stages. When you reach a level of strength in your leadership, you'll know it because it feels as if you're firing on all cylinders. It's awesome. The reality is that we have to pursue the ideal even when we aren't hitting the target. Having too much confidence should not be a top worry. Lacking confidence should.

I'm convinced there are three main ways to build confidence.

1. Lay a Biblical Foundation for Your Confidence

While confidence is critical to good leadership, misplaced confidence will eventually turn against you. Paul stated boldly that God called him as an apostle. He wasn't saying that he was confident in his ability to pull off apostleship. Instead, he was saying God called him, so he was then free to travel the known world as an apostle of Christ.

This might seem too obvious to mention, but it's far from obvious. Our culture makes it difficult to believe in things unseen. Rather than putting our faith in the unchanging truth of God, today's culture would have us trust only the things we can see, hear, and touch.

We can't see God, but we certainly sense His calling. That sense of calling is as real as anything else, but it's not a signed contract on file at the county recorder's office. Still, Paul didn't hesitate to follow God's call even though his best-known achievements prior to this were as a standout Pharisee working to rid the world of Jesus followers. It's true that Paul had encountered Jesus in a vision and had been blinded as a result. But that didn't serve as proof to everyone (see Acts 9:13).

Paul held to his calling, and over time he became the greatest first-century leader after Jesus Christ. His past, his previous violent work against the church, and his long years of training as a Pharisee didn't cause him to lack confidence in his role as a leader of the church and missionary to the Gentiles.

What about other giants of the faith? Hebrews 11 reminds us of Abraham, Moses, David, and others whose names thousands of years later still define brilliant leadership. And every one of them led from a place of faith. They trusted that their obedience and focus on honoring God would not be in vain, even if they didn't see the promised fruit in their lifetimes.

Then the author of Hebrews drops this amazing truth on us:

> Do you see what this means—all these pioneers who blazed the way, all these veterans cheering us on? It means we'd better get on with it. Strip down, start running—and never quit! No extra spiritual fat, no parasitic sins. Keep your eyes on *Jesus,* who both began and finished this race we're in. Study how he did it. Because he never lost sight of where he was headed—that exhilarating finish in and with God—he could put up with anything along the way: Cross, shame, whatever. And now he's *there,* in the place of honor, right alongside God. When you find yourselves flagging in your faith, go over that story again, item by item, that long litany of hostility he plowed through. *That* will shoot adrenaline into your souls! (12:1–3, MSG)

The reason I use Scripture as the foundation of my confidence is because people saw and recorded that Jesus predicted His death, was killed, and then was raised from the dead three days later. He is worthy of our trust. When we keep our eyes on Jesus, we see people the way we are supposed to. We know to see people as His mission to love the world. That builds our confidence in how He wants to partner with us.

Take a minute to create a simple historical evaluation of your experiences with God.

- Have you experienced God in tangible ways throughout your life and leadership? If so (and I hope you can answer in the affirmative), when and how have you experienced Him?
- Describe a time when God moved in your life in an unexpected way.
- What about a time when God was faithful to you in the way we see His faithfulness to Abraham, Moses, David, the prophets, and others in Scripture? Give a summary of God's faithfulness to you.

You build confidence over time. You gain confidence after seeing something prove to be trustworthy and true time and time again. Your golf swing. Your fly-fishing casting ability. Your artistic expression. Your skills as a parent. Your exercise routine producing greater health in your body and in your life.

All are confidence builders. When you trust that the principles in Scripture are true and that they work, your confidence grows. Your belief in what God says is true. Moreover, your understanding of what God says about you becomes true to you on an experiential level. That's when you start to crack the code on confidence.

2. Trust Your Strengths

Over the past couple of decades, discovering strengths has become quite the subject for writers and thought leaders. Author, speaker, and leadership guru John Maxwell has spoken at length about the importance of working from within your strengths. Leadership expert Marcus Buckingham has written books that help leaders discover their strengths so they can operate from a basis of strength. Pastor Andy Stanley has taught on the topic of leaning into your strengths to lead at your very best.

I'll add my support to their approach to strengths. If you haven't already, begin your search for your own strengths. Learn who you are. It will help you uncover the strengths God gave you to be used in fulfilling His call on your life. Only then can you lead from your truest self. When you are operating in your strengths most of the time, you will be energized and efficient.

As leaders and team builders, we have to put leaders in positions that are life-giving for them. That means matching roles and responsibilities to the leaders' strengths. There is no job in the world in which you can operate fully within your strengths, but team builders need to keep an applicant's strengths in the forefront when hiring. If a staff member operates half the time or more out of learned behavior rather than inherent strengths, that person will be continually exhausted.

Life-giving leaders understand how important this is for their success and for the success of the people for whom they are responsible. You need to protect your people and your team from operating outside of their gifting for extended periods of time. They can do what's necessary for a season, but long term it will lead to ineffectiveness and exhaustion. So does all this mean you can disregard your weaknesses? I wish, but no.

3. Grow in Your Weaknesses

This is the part where I like to veer off the chapter outline and launch into a side discussion. I understand where Maxwell, Buckingham, and Stanley are coming from with regard to leading from your strengths. It's just as important as they say it is. However, as we lead from our strengths, we also *have* to pay attention to our weaknesses.

I know leaders who use a personality assessment as a crutch. They read avidly about their strengths and decide their strengths will cancel out or overwhelm their weaknesses. Such an assumption allows them to avoid working on the areas in which they need to grow.

"I'm not good at doing that, so I'll find someone else to do it for me."
"I can't do that because it's not one of my strengths." Often the tasks are
left unattended, which causes problems later on.

We can never let our desire to operate in our strengths keep us from
doing our jobs—meaning everything our jobs entail. No job will have you
leading only in areas of your personal strength.

For example, I'm a highly relational leader. I'm categorized as an en-
courager on the RightPath assessment, an ESFP on the Myers-Briggs Type
Indicator, and "Woo" in StrengthsFinder. Basically, I'm all about people,
people, people.

I won't try to argue that highly relational leaders are low in structure,
but many can be. That has been my story. I have to work hard to get better
at structure and details. My team knows I will never be a great organizer,
planner, and detail checker. But I can get better.

Here's where I differ with the prevailing thinking on strengths versus
weaknesses. I believe your strengths are natural to you. They don't require
a ton of thinking or extra effort. You operate with the benefit of your
strengths because that's who you are. It would be strange to do otherwise.
You don't have to debate which way to go—results or relationships. Just do
what comes naturally to you.

On the other hand, your weaknesses force you to think differently.
For example, when I go into an event week, if I focus on communicating
details well to my team, I'll improve in that area. And while I'm improving
on an area of weakness, I never worry that I'll somehow forget to be relational. You might be off-the-charts organized, but if you focus on people
(if that's a weakness for you), don't worry that you'll suddenly lose track of
the details.

Life-giving leaders don't try to turn a weakness into a strength, but
they work hard to know their weaknesses and improve them. They strive
to become well-balanced. I don't love working in Excel, but I have to. I

can't just assume other staff members will pick it up for me. I will never take a job in which Excel becomes central to my daily work, but I can't avoid it completely.

Confidence without arrogance builds trust for your leadership in the people around you, and it builds trust within yourself. Life-giving leaders who are confident without being arrogant will make the leaders around them better because of trust.

What About You?

In which areas do you lack confidence? Could it be that you have not found confidence in your calling? Before you turn to the next chapter, ask God to meet with you and allow you to participate in an Upstairs conversation. Maybe you need to look back over your strengths and weaknesses and develop a simple plan to lean into your strengths and grow in your weaknesses.

Take a minute and write down five areas in which you lack confidence. Financial management? Leading other leaders? Technology upgrades? Fund-raising? New business development? Fear of the unknown?

If you need additional professional training in an area, figure out what that looks like. Start practicing confidence in a few areas you're uncertain about. Take all these roles to the Lord and ask for His help to grow in these capacities.

Confidence is a game changer. And while confidence is weakened by arrogance, it is possible to act upon the confidence of your calling without assuming it has anything to do with personal merit or that you somehow earned it. A calling comes from God, according to His will, not ours.

Confidence has to exist without arrogance. But how do you do that? I'm so glad you asked.

8

Something Bigger

Life-Giving Leaders Are Humble

I haven't always been the physical specimen I am now. Just FYI. I grew up in Georgia and played soccer my entire life. During spring, summer, fall, and winter, I was playing soccer somewhere. I was always the youngest member of my team. (Because I was born in June, I started school about a year earlier than the other kids in my class.)

What's it like for the youngest kid in school when he's in class, on the soccer field, or in any other setting? I was capable from an academic and social perspective (I hope you hear the sarcasm in my writing), but my physical stature was an issue. I was usually the smallest. Somebody had to be the short kid, and I never thought much about it until I started high school.

My freshman year I weighed ninety-three pounds and was five feet four. Most people thought either "That's cute!" or "So what if he's small?" But for me—a boy trying to become a man—being small wasn't a good thing. My personality allowed me to be seen, but my physique did not.

And another thing: when you're a fourteen-year-old boy, you don't want to be called cute.

Things got worse. In ninth grade I was cut from the soccer team. All the guys I had played with for years made the team; I didn't. I was heartbroken. I knew I could play on the same field with those guys because we had made the same teams together for years. The thing is, by my freshman year, they were bigger than I was.

What was I to do with all the time I suddenly had on my hands?

My PE teacher was Coach Woods. He was a great teacher, and I loved being around him. He was also the wrestling coach. One day he said he needed another wrestler for the junior varsity team in the 103-pound weight class. That's the lowest weight class. (Some tournaments had a 95-pound division, which would really make my weekend.)

I had never wrestled a day in my life, other than with my older brother. But when Coach Woods approached me about going out for wrestling, I thought, *Why not?*

Wrestling was the hardest thing I'd ever done. I have never been more humbled than when I wrestled. The season had already started when I joined the team, but I'm a quick study—or so I thought. I had been a wrestler for only two weeks when the first match came around. All ninety-three pounds of me was mentally ready. I was a small package of twisted steel, and I came ready to battle. New wrestling shoes glistened at the ends of my toothpick legs. I might be the only wrestler in history whose singlet (the spandex wrestling outfit) was loose. Yet I was ready. Let's go.

The 103-pound weight class is always the first match to be held. Then it goes up from there all the way to the heavyweights. I would set the tone for my team's wrestlers. That day we were wrestling Parkview High School, our rivals. What could be better?

In sports, Parkview tended to beat us at everything. Even today, my wife, who is a Parkview alum, reminds me of her school's dominance. My school, Shiloh, had a good wrestling team, but Parkview was better.

Sure, Parkview was powerful. But their team had never encountered the short beast about to be unleashed on their wrestling team. I warmed up to Metallica's "Enter Sandman." I bounced around and loosened my muscles. They were like strings on a guitar (and you know how thin guitar strings are). If you played them right, watch out.

The whistle blew and my opponent and I walked to the middle of the mat. I was in black. He was in orange. I stood there and looked at Ronnie Stevens. I'll never forget his name, mainly because he went on to become a state champion. There was also the thing that happened next.

I shook hands with Ronnie. Sixteen seconds later we were both standing and the referee was raising Ronnie's hand for some reason. The epic battle was apparently over and I wasn't even breathing deeply. I can't remember what happened during the match except that I was on my back so fast the referee had to hurry to slap the mat. We shook hands, and we walked off the mat. My chance at a perfect season was gone. Well, at least in the win category. I did end that season with a perfect season, though: 0–8.

At times life humbles you. Obviously your response determines whether you become humbled or angry. Ronnie Stevens and the next seven wrestlers I faced that year were used to teach me humility. Many of those guys had wrestled for years; I had wrestled for weeks. I was turned down by girls I asked out on dates. I've applied for jobs that were given to other applicants. Every now and then you get knocked off the artificial pedestal you've put yourself on. And it's a good thing.

Humility is a teacher that will change your life. But learning from it is brutally difficult.

On the other hand, humility is a daily choice. It doesn't have to be a lesson learned because of harsh circumstances. The decision is yours. You can choose to see life from a humble posture or from a posture of arrogance.

Here's the crazy part of my high school story: I kept coming back. Not because I was going to be a state champion, but because I was part of something bigger than myself. I was on a team. They needed me. They at least needed a chance to have a win in my weight class. (I wrestled three years and got better at it. I also grew eight inches and gained weight.) When you put something that's bigger than yourself ahead of yourself, you are choosing humility.

Your life and effort become about something else and someone else. You live according to a different standard of measure.

WHAT IS HUMILITY?

Humility is the only step in the process of becoming a life-giving leader in which you make the choice to focus on something outside yourself and your personality. It is the additional influence to your leadership legacy that just might make the largest impact. There might be people who are naturally wired to be humble. But even so, I would say humility is always a choice a person has to make.

Does humility mean you're a doormat or a passive observer? Not at all.

Humility doesn't mean you're a pushover.

Humility doesn't mean you don't pursue achievement.

Humility doesn't mean you're worthless.

Humility isn't the same as meekness.

Humility doesn't require you to beat yourself up if you want something for yourself.

Humility isn't weakness.

Humility isn't having a reserved personality.

As Rick Warren said, "Humility is not thinking less of yourself; it's thinking of yourself less."[1]

Humility involves choosing to live for something bigger than yourself. Instead of concerning yourself with only your personal circle, you expand it to include other people around you. For followers of Jesus, I see humility as the choice to allow God to take center stage in your life. When you live for something bigger and that is Jesus, humility will be an overflow of your relationship with Him.

THE ROOTS OF HUMILITY

As the writer of Proverbs observed, "Wisdom's instruction is to fear the LORD, and *humility* comes before honor" (15:33, NIV). The world we live in disagrees. It clamors for respect more than almost anything else.

People demand respect for their position, their wealth, and their abilities. But respect isn't the thing to pursue; humility is.

When the Bible mentions "to fear the Lord," it is referring to understanding God's proper place. He is above all and in all. You hold God with appropriate standing. You put God above all. Humility calls for us to comprehend what God is capable of.

The fear of the Lord is a healthy fear. It's similar to understanding the power of a moving train, an active volcano, or a hurricane. You need to have a healthy fear of their massive power. You don't want to be paralyzed by the fear but rather allow the fear to bring a proper perspective. If you don't respect and fear the power of a hurricane, for instance, prepare to suffer the consequences.

Likewise, not having a healthy fear of God's ability and power will affect your life down the road.

Fearing the Lord allows us to get a small measure of perspective on how humility works. It's an opportunity for us to realize there's something at play other than ourselves. There is much more going on than what's happening in your world or mine. Choosing to be humble doesn't prevent you from achieving or from being successful. I believe the verse we looked at from Proverbs 15 says the opposite: "Wisdom's instruction is to fear the

LORD, and *humility* comes before honor" (verse 33, NIV). You will be honored when you choose humility.

In the New Testament, we find another way to view humility in our lives. Look at what Romans 12:3 (NIV) explains: "Do not think of yourself more highly than you ought, but rather think of yourself with sober judgment, in accordance with the faith God has distributed to each of you."

Humility is a choice to appreciate God's gifts in your life, but with sober judgment. Paul went on to talk about how each of us is a different part of one body. We are one, but we have different gifts and jobs. When you are part of a team, you have to rely on the other parts to serve the greater purpose.

I've seen interviews with successful athletes who barely acknowledge their teammates. After huge wins, the athletes talk about themselves and their contributions to the victory. You can have a good game, but you don't even have a game without the other players. It's refreshing to see players who get that. I much prefer to hear from team members who understand they play as a team, not as individuals. Humility reminds us we can't do it ourselves.

It's one thing to understand your role as part of a larger whole. But what about in your life, your world, and your job? Because we are Jesus followers, humility should become second nature to us. We believe that God is above all and in all. He's sovereign over our lives. When we put our faith and trust in Jesus, we are committing to live for a new name. It means we think of ourselves less and think of God and others more.

Be confident in your work as you serve others but remain humble. Understand and celebrate your uniqueness as you keep it under God's authority and within His plan.

Why did I add humility to this list of life-giving qualities? What does humility look like in practice? How does being humble play out on a daily basis? How do we know if we're doing it correctly? Let's see if we can discover characteristics of humility that can guide our leadership.

HUMILITY PAVES THE WAY FOR TRUST

It's a simple question: Is it easier to trust someone who is arrogant or someone who is humble? Whom would you rather work for: leaders who are convinced they are the reason for the success of the team or leaders who develop others and make them the reason for the team's success?

Humble leaders attract people. Humble leaders position themselves in ways to make the team around them better. Life-giving leaders, whether at the top of the organization or the bottom, use their perspective to call others to higher leadership. Here are a few ways to pursue humility as a life-giving leader.

Be Intentional

Leaders who embody humility are intentional about it. Humility doesn't happen haphazardly. Leaders who develop it are intentional about putting other people first. They live for something bigger than themselves.

Nothing happens consistently without consistent pursuit. I can't tell you how many people I've heard tell about what will happen when they win the lottery or get a great job. When people leave their lives to chance, they never make real progress. Likewise, humility doesn't just happen. You have to work for it. You choose it every moment, and it's one of the best choices you can make.

What if you said a simple prayer every morning that gets your heart in the proper posture? For example, "Lord, may I walk in step with Your Spirit today. Help me keep the proper perspective. Thank You for making me unique, and may I use my special design to make those around me better. Amen."

A palms-up approach to the day can keep humility at the forefront, because a simple action such as turning your hands up to God is a physical representation of an internal posture. This doesn't just happen. You have to be intentional.

Learn to Receive

As I have mentioned, if you can't receive encouragement, appreciation, or gifts from others, it can work against the humility you're trying to build. As leaders, we have to learn how to honor the people around us.

Here's the best guardrail I've put in place to maintain proper perspective while learning to receive gifts: I remind myself they are gifts and not something owed to me. When gifts go from being gifts to being something you think you deserve, you start losing the humility battle.

A while ago my wife and I were invited to attend an event in Los Angeles. It turned out to be awesome and the accommodations were exceptional—beyond anything we've stayed at before. The view of Hollywood was incredible. The food was amazing. And we enjoyed being driven around in a car that had a "B with wings" (my wife's words—it was a Bentley).

After two days I really started to feel as if I was somebody. It was as if I deserved to stay at luxury hotels all the time (whether I can afford them or not).

If you're not careful, gifts can create dissatisfaction with other places or things in your life. You know what I'm talking about. You're invited to speak out of state and your host puts you up in the basic hotel chain you've stayed at a million times. It stings a little. You may not want to admit it, but you know you were expecting something better.

Humility starts to erode as soon as you feel as if you deserve the gift. Life-giving leaders learn to see gifts as gifts rather than as payment. Maintaining that perspective is crucial to staying humble.

Gratitude Is the Best Attitude

When you lose gratitude, you learn poor attitude. It's as simple as that. Here's a dictionary definition of *attitude:* "A settled way of thinking or feeling about someone or something, typically one that is reflected in a person's behavior."[2]

That is an important definition. Your way of thinking turns into be-havior, and it dictates the way you respond. Right thinking will get you started on the right foot in any situation. The reverse is true as well. If you start with negative thinking, it will result in negative behavior. You cannot assume you will automatically shift back into correct thinking just before the rubber meets the road.

If you keep gratefulness at the center of your thinking, you will see an attitude of gratitude. Humility will follow, and you will be thankful. Who doesn't want to work for a leader who is thankful for what you do?

Leaders, I know some of you sign your employees' checks, but they aren't your personal paychecks that you're handing over. And your em-ployees are not your private supply of team members. Any one of them—or all of them—could choose to work somewhere else at any time. They choose to work with you, and your sincere expressions of gratitude can keep them around as well as keep them thriving in their jobs.

What if this week you chose gratitude with the people around you? How would that instantly change your organization? Write a thank-you note today. Stop by and thank someone.

I brought up humility toward the end of this process because it really is the culmination of the first steps in the process. When you become a life-giving leader, your awareness, acceptance, and confidence allow you to keep your wits about you. They allow you to be proud of who God made you to be and where He has brought you. We are called to be lights in this world (see Luke 11:33). Lights stand out in the darkness, and God wants His people to be seen—to stand out—in contrast to the surrounding darkness. Arrogance also allows you to be seen. The difference is that when you operate out of arrogance, other people don't see you as a light.

Humility changes the game for leaders and makes you a light. So many leaders talk about how to have an influence on the workplace that points to Jesus. Humility is so countercultural that people take notice when they see it. Humble leaders are rare, and they give people a perfect connection to the bigger story: the story of God and His work. The pathway to life-giving leadership is paved with humility.

What About You?

Imagine a workplace filled with humility. Imagine a business in which leaders are trying to outserve one another instead of competing with one another. Imagine a staff that chooses to push others forward because they believe in something bigger than themselves.

I know these examples sound idealized, and maybe they are. But you have a role to play in making humble leadership a reality. Where could you see yourself working to make sure the mission is the focus and not you and your efforts? Where could you help push someone else to the front? In what ways have you become too competitive lately, and how can you return to humility rather than buying into the rule of competition? It takes special leaders to live and lead this way. It calls for surrendering and trusting the Lord big-time. We will talk more about this in a few chapters.

To do this well, you have to be healthy. As we finish surveying the streams that join your leadership to grow your influence, we finish with health. Life-giving leaders are healthy leaders.

9

At the Top of Your Game

Life-Giving Leaders Are Healthy

Health is a prerequisite for life-giving leadership. It's just that simple and concrete.

I don't believe most leaders set out to be unhealthy. Still, the number of leaders who have to take a break because of burnout and such seems to grow each year. Maybe they feel it's similar to a budget: sometimes you don't pay attention to it until you've hit a breaking point. Stress, travel, and the constant demands of business tend to keep us from finding the consistency in health that we need for the long haul.

I'll be the first to admit I'm not always the picture of health. I like to drink Coca-Cola. It's seriously my favorite thing. It's a terrible beverage if a healthy diet is your goal, and I'm working on cutting back. But I also really like the new Crispy M&M's. I don't exercise as much as I should. Having kids makes life a little more complicated. Nonetheless, I know how important it is to be active. As I write this chapter, I'm planning a couple of specific deep dives into getting healthier. I'm pretty active, but I know I need a plan. Disciplined adjustments to diet and exercise are critical.

Good health can help protect us from burnout. And yet it's still tough for me to avoid soft drinks, lower my caffeine intake, and eat gluten-free.

The alternative is way worse. Who wants to become another statistic representing another leader lost to ministry and mission because he or she preferred to take an unhealthy route? I'm tired of losing church leaders to moral failure exacerbated by burnout and accelerated by terrible decisions. I'm not excusing their poor decisions, but I believe healthy leaders make better decisions, including the decision to stay away from career-ending choices.

When the leader is well, the team can tell.

I'm sure you know someone who is crazy talented and amazingly competent but fizzled out of leadership because he or she was unhealthy outside of work. I hate it, but it happens more often than we'd like to say. If you're running on empty, you have nothing to give. The car stops moving when there's no gas in the tank, regardless of the engine's capacity and potential. A Ferrari will go nowhere without gas.

I asked pastor and author Craig Groeschel what motivated him to stay as fit as he is. He said taking care of his body became a spiritual issue for him. He wanted to honor God with his body so he could do what God has in store for him. It was a heart issue, not a body issue.

Life-giving leaders have to be healthy and filled with life to give life away. Easier said than done, right?

There is zero chance I can hit all the areas of health in this chapter, so I'm going to hit on the five I believe will help leaders stay healthy. With a little time and attention, these components of health will have you humming on all cylinders and leading people the way you were made to lead. And by the way, I'm writing this for myself as much as for you. I know how important this is. You know how important this is. Health never takes a vacation. We have to remember it requires our best.

BOUNDARIES

If you want to leave a lasting legacy, you have to learn the importance of creating and upholding boundaries. Legendary stories are told about leaders such as Billy Graham who created boundaries early on to avoid being alone with any woman other than his wife. I'm not saying this has to be your rule, but the famous evangelist drew a line in the sand to create a boundary. He knew his ministry and integrity depended on maintaining wise boundaries. Many leaders create financial boundaries for their organizations that keep them from making bad short-term decisions. Enforcing margin percentages for profit, clear accountability regarding investments, and even spending freezes when appropriate are common for organizations and leaders trying to get or stay healthy.

No matter how long it took you to gain influence, it will take only a moment to lose it. That's scary and true. Integrity demands constant attention. It requires you to fight for intentional boundaries and understandings. As the famous poet Keith Urban wrote, "Gone tomorrow, here today."[1] It takes very little time to lose influence and a long time to gain it.

If you put in years of effort to become a life-giving leader, why wouldn't you put boundaries in place to protect your work and your reputation? I cannot emphasize this enough. Boundaries will protect you and your influence.

Here are a few boundaries I have established:

- I will not travel with, meet with, eat a meal with, or ride in a car alone with a woman (except for my wife and other family members). If I need to travel for work with a female staff member, I pay to have a third person travel with us.

When I have one-on-one meetings with a woman, we meet in an office with windows so people can see in. I set this standard based on what I learned over the years at other organizations, and it has never let me down. When the team understands this concept and works to implement it, it's not awkward.

- I also keep a rule regarding gossip. If someone talks with me about an issue with someone at work, my first question is, "Have you already talked with that person?" If the answer is no, then we stop the meeting until the wronged party has spoken with the other person face to face. Everyone on the team knows this rule. It creates a culture that tries to eliminate gossip.

- Last, I keep consistent work hours so the team knows that I try to leave the office by four thirty every day, if possible. This allows me time with my wife and kids. It allows the team to create hours for themselves. I'm almost always the first one in, so it's not a question of the amount of time worked. Instead, it's a matter of creating clear boundaries to protect my time with my family.

Which brings me to my next point.

RHYTHM

I have debated whether a balance between work and life is possible. I agree that having the two wildly out of balance is damaging, but the word *balance* is problematic. I propose we think of it as seeking a rhythm of work and life.

For many of us the idea of work/life balance suggests equal playing time. The reality is that if you work more than forty hours per week, if you get the recommended amount of sleep, if you travel for work and run errands and get together with friends and get regular exercise in your free time, there is no way that time spent with your family can equal the time you spend away from your family. Rather than balance, then, we are shooting for a work/life rhythm. We can plan for the rhythm and flow of our seasons.

In my work we have very busy spring and fall seasons. They are the best times to hold events. December is a terrible time for any event other than Christmas, so we close the office for two weeks during this slower time. We use the time away from the office to recover and prepare for the next season. It's a rhythm.

After an event week I want my team to have time to recover. This is something I have to model. I want my team and my family to see me work hard and then prioritize my relationships when the intense work season has passed. When you have downtime, try to recover. Spend extra time with family, friends, and yourself. When you're in a crazy season, make sure the boundaries you have in place keep you focused and away from the burnout danger zone.

Rhythm is found in how you approach your days and work in general. Clear expectations with family and communication in advance can help curb the sting of long, tiring work hours.

FRIENDS

If there was ever an area that requires health, it's relationships with friends. Over the past few years, I've been paying attention to older leaders. One of the areas I look at is their friendships. Do they have any close friends? Do they have people they can talk to when they need advice? Are they lonelier than young leaders?

As an extrovert, I have more than one best friend. (If you're an introvert, I want you to know it's okay to have more than one. In fact, it takes some pressure off your one best friend if you add a few more to the mix.)

Two of my best friends were my college roommates. They have been trusted buddies for more than twenty years. These guys, Steve Hambrick and Ashley Hill, have been amazingly close to me. They have cared for me, loved me, laughed with *and* at me, and have stuck with me no matter what. Steve's dad once asked us, "Do you guys realize how special your friendship is? I don't have many close friends, and I wish I had what you guys have. Make sure you cherish it." He's right. Friendships are foundational for great lives and great leaders.

Life-giving leaders also give life to their friends, and their friends should be a reservoir of grace and life for the leaders. I've seen older leaders who have no close friends. It breaks my heart. When you are alone or feel alone, you see the highs and lows of life as extremely high or low. When you have close friends, though, they help you regulate your perception and understanding of all sorts of things. Highs and lows, successes and failures, progressions and stalemates.

You have to invite people into your life, and that requires an investment of time, energy, and emotion. Healthy friendships do not exist on a one-way street. Men seem to have a harder time with this, but it's not exclusive to men. The power that comes from great friendships will fuel you for a lifetime if you steward your friendships well.

Leadership requires friendships. No job is worth giving up your friendships.

HOBBIES

Raise your hand if you just took a deep sigh. Here it comes, yet another author telling you it's wrong to neglect your worthwhile hobbies.

Wrong. I'm a leader telling you, a leader, that you have to have *great* hobbies. Dr. Sam Chand discussed stress with our staff. I can't recreate his statement word-for-word, but he basically said, "Stress is going to go somewhere. Either you decide where it goes or it will decide. If you let stress find its own relief, you will lose every time."[2]

Stress has to be relieved somehow. You can pick the means of relief, or you can let stress find an outlet. Often when stress chooses the path of relief, it turns a leader's small problems into an addiction. It turns simple fatigue and frustration into an out-of-control issue. It allows a small amount of debt to balloon into a daunting financial burden.

Hobbies are a great way to relieve stress in a healthy way. If you play golf and get so angry after a poor shot that you throw your clubs, maybe that's not the best hobby for you. If you lose patience or get stressed out because of a hobby, find a better hobby. For some it's writing. For many it's art. For you it might be yard work, crafts, or fishing.

My only suggestion is that you should find a hobby (or hobbies) that can take your attention and mind elsewhere. If you have a hobby that's not interesting enough or compelling enough to take your mind off your work, you're missing the point of having a hobby. Golf works for me. It's one of my only activities that forces me to think about things that have nothing to do with work. It takes me outdoors, it's competitive, and I can play with family and friends.

What hobby works for you?

EXERCISE

It wouldn't be a conversation about health without talking about diet and exercise. Let's set diet aside for now and focus on exercise. Scripture is pretty clear: "Do you not know that your bodies are temples of the Holy Spirit, who is in you, whom you have received from God? You are not your own; you were bought at a price. Therefore honor God with your bodies" (1 Corinthians 6:19–20, NIV).

The context of this verse has to do with how intimacy with other people affects more than just your body. But the verse also paints a clear picture that honoring God means protecting and taking care of your body. (As I wrote that sentence, I realized how much I was slouching at my desk.) We need to be intentional about taking care of our bodies so we can use them to glorify God and bring life to others.

Is anyone going to argue against having a healthy body? No one wants to be sick or weak, short of breath, short on energy, or unable to do normal things such as carrying bags of groceries, climbing up and down a ladder, or swinging an ax to cut down a small tree. When you exercise, it's better for your body, better for your mind, and better for your leadership legacy. You will not have a long-term leadership legacy if you don't take care of your body, and exercise plays an essential role in doing that.

Your body is created for exercise. Endorphins, hormones, muscles, adrenaline, and all your different bodily functions work best when they are put to use. You need to move and be active so your mind and body can function at a high capacity. You have had plenty of days of sitting at a desk, sitting in meetings, sitting at lunch, sitting on the couch and watching movies. For a variety of reasons we devote ourselves to not moving, and then we're surprised when we feel lethargic. Our bodies were made for exercise. Get your body moving and your leadership will be energized.

Leaders, on which of these five areas do you need to focus your attention over the next seven days? Pick one. Make one step in the right direction in one of these areas. Your leadership is too important not to do this. Today is a better day to start than tomorrow. Let's go.

Part 3

Core Behaviors of Life-Giving Leaders

It's time to shift gears. Now that we understand how to lead from our truest selves, we can turn our attention outward. The life-giving understanding of leadership lets us care for those in our circle of influence with everything we have. Once we have identified our natural wiring and are developing as life-giving leaders, how do we develop the behaviors of a life-giving leader?

As life-giving leaders, we accept a call to four life-giving principles. Honestly, the principles we'll look at in the next four chapters should make up the DNA of all Jesus followers. Life-giving leaders learn to be consistent with these principles at home and at work. It's not an add-on but a way of living that is ingrained in us, anchored deep in our hearts. Leaders embrace the call to let life flow from them by allowing these four callings to infiltrate their lives.

Great leaders change the world by allowing the power of leadership to push them daily. These principles challenge leaders to be sharper and more productive. They push us to care for others with intentionality and skill. Once the fire is lit in our souls, leadership that gives life to others becomes the focus of our work.

Life-giving leaders embrace these four calls:

- A call to sweat
- A call to sacrifice
- A call to surrender
- A call to serve

While you read this section, keep an eye out for the direction of life flow. You will see these four behaviors flow out of a life that God is pouring into. God pours life into you, and you pass life on to the people around you.

As we look at each of these, I pray that God will nudge you in the area He will use to give your leadership an upgrade.

10

A Call to Sweat

Life-Giving Leaders Work Selflessly

My dad has been a mechanic for as long as I can remember. I have watched him sweat like crazy while working in garages on every type of engine. He can figure out how anything works. If he doesn't know something, he learns more about it and then works hard to fill the gap.

I've watched him pull carburetors, clean them, rebuild them if necessary, and reinstall them. He does that whether he has worked on a particular type of car before or not. He is one of the hardest working men I've ever known. It wasn't until recently I realized what a gift he has given me in modeling the call to sweat.

Hard work and sweat are often the hallmarks of great leaders. This should come as no surprise, but some of the most meaningful principles are right in front of us and we still miss them. On the other hand, we all know leaders who want to be great but aren't willing to put in the practice and work it takes.

I know many of you must be thinking, *Really? A call to sweat? That's pretty gross.* When you grow up in the South, you get used to sweating. But what I'm talking about is a call to work hard. To sweat alongside your team. To dive in and make sure there's nothing you would ask of your team that you would not be willing to do yourself.

This past year I decided to coach both of my sons' flag football teams. You want to talk about sweating? I'm not sure I've ever sweat so much in my life. We would have an hour-long practice and an hour-long game. And in Georgia you sweat just leaving your garage. Since I was devoting two hours to a practice and a game for each of my two sons, I'd spend four hours in the sun losing seven thousand calories per minute. Okay, that might be a slight overstatement, but I wish it were true.

Do you know why I do this? I might ask that question myself. I don't have time to coach flag football. And rather than coach the teams, I'd love to be able to sit back and watch the games. However, embracing a call to sweat and a desire to make an impact does not allow me to sit on the sideline. The long hours required to coach kids on top of an already busy schedule could have kept me from agreeing to take on this opportunity. I'm not saying I have a lot to offer when it comes to coaching flag football (even though I did play in the finals of the University of Georgia flag football championship and went on to play at halftime of an Atlanta Falcons game. Just saying).

But I was there, in the sun, sweating. I was doing my best to think of some crazy plays. Trying to coach kids who might never play again. Trying to teach them how to deal with failure. Trying to exemplify how to work hard. Trying to show them that each kid matters and that an adult other than their parents cares about them and their character. These lessons can't be taught unless a leader accepts the call to sweat and the call to work hard.

You never know when your hard work will pay off. Obviously, being able to watch my boys play is a great highlight of coaching, but there was a certain moment that assured me that I made the right decision.

One of the boys on my younger son's team was new to the sport. If you were to ask me at the beginning of the season who would require the majority of my coaching time, I'd have named this kid. I'll admit that I found his lack of ability and short attention span a little frustrating.

Then, one Saturday, in the middle of the season, we were practicing prior to a game. I struck up a conversation with this boy's dad, and he made a passing comment that changed my heart. The dad said he had never seen his son love anything more than playing flag football that season. He'd played different sports, but nothing had affected him as our football team did.

What?

Are we talking about the same child? The one who doesn't know where to run or what a wide receiver is?

I was floored. But then I saw it. Shiny eyes. Joy. Love. Fun.

Then I thought about the life-giving leadership callings I've taught about for years.

Life-giving leadership does not happen when you're sitting on the sideline either at work or on the field. Engaging in hard work will always bear fruit. It just does. No matter your role in an organization, when you see the people around you get shiny eyes, it changes you. Every time. Just as with coaching kids. It keeps you coming back. It makes everyone in the building better. It makes you better.

The flow of life that comes from you doesn't happen when you're looking at another person's leadership. It happens when *you* lead. Sitting on the sideline and watching someone else lead will cause you to regret a missed opportunity to make a difference. Choosing to disengage when the work is hard or requires us to sweat usually leads to regret. Choosing the easy route never gets you to the best destination.

Listen, leader. Hard work will *always* be a requirement of life-giving leadership.

We all know that hard work gets a bad rap. The millennial generation, members of which make up most of my team, has been given the blanket stereotype of entitlement. In this case, the word *entitlement* is code for lazy. I don't know about you, but I can't think of a word that could be more harmful to the church than *lazy*.

Often the best leadership quotes can be found on bumper stickers. One of my favorites is "Hard work has a future payoff; laziness pays off now." Success and leadership require massive amounts of sweat and hustle.

To all you millennials, when you're given a label or stereotype you didn't earn, you have to go twice as far in the other direction to change the label. It's not fair, and the label falls far short of describing the millennials I know. On the other hand, some legitimate reasoning lies behind the label.

Leadership expert Simon Sinek recently talked about millennials at a Catalyst event: "No empathy. They say that you're unleadable. They say they don't understand you. They say that your generation is different and has different priorities. . . . Nonsense. I think you're misunderstood."[1]

He went on to explain that part of what contributes to a stereotype is the way the targeted demographic cohort was parented. For instance, if members of this generation were not taught to delay gratification when they were young, how are they supposed to practice this skill of adulthood once they grow up? You don't get a promotion at work based on having positioned yourself well on social media. Instant gratification does not apply to getting ahead at work or ensuring career satisfaction.

The answer is to sweat more. Hard work breaks the chains of instant gratification. The process defines a person's impact, not his or her destination. You have to dig in. Long hours, heavy lifting, and dirty hands are required for life-giving leadership.

If you have been judged unfairly based on an inaccurate stereotype, you work your tail off to create a new perception. The process of sweating to get the job done, without cutting corners, will define your legacy.

How much more would you stand out in your organization if you chose to be the opposite of your generational label? What if you are the hardest-working person in the building? What if your leaders recognized that you didn't think you knew everything but instead asked questions and wanted to learn everything? What if your reputation were saturated with accolades of a positive work ethic? What if you were the first one to move boxes, clean up the break room, or organize the supply closet? Hiring managers know that those qualities in an employee quickly take the person from the middle of the pack to the top.

The reason I kicked off the list of leadership behaviors with sweat is because I believe the millennial generation and the generation following will begin to break this stereotype of entitlement. When you choose to work your tail off, the world notices. The gospel can change the world with a committed group of hardworking believers. It's Leadership 101.

One of my favorite Martin Luther King Jr. speeches is about working hard in every area of your life: "If a man is called to be a street sweeper, he should sweep streets even as a Michelangelo painted or Beethoven composed music or Shakespeare wrote poetry. He should sweep streets so well that all the hosts of heaven and earth will pause to say, 'Here lived a great street sweeper who did his job well.'"[2]

LONG HOURS

Mark Cuban, owner of the Dallas Mavericks and a tech genius, once said, "Work like there is someone working 24 hours a day to take it all away from you."[3]

As I'm writing this, I'm also working overtime because we are in our busiest season. Catalyst is an event organization, so the spring and fall seasons are crazy. During some event weeks we work eighteen-hour days. And we love it. We spend the whole year planning for these events, so why wouldn't we love the hard work needed to make the events happen? Any time a new staff member joins the team, I explain to him or her that no matter your title, once we get to the event site, we all become part of the operations team. We all work to move pallets and furniture, create great guest experiences, pack boxes, put out fires, and take on all the other execution items.

When I think of long hours, I think about my accountant. I have received emails from him at one in the morning. CPAs embrace long hours from December to May. It's part of the job. They can't cut corners or take shortcuts. They have to be all in.

The same is true with life-giving leaders. The greatest leaders never cut corners. They dig in when long hours are required. In every occupation some seasons are busier than others. Educators have assessments, lawyers have trial seasons, bankers have audits, and ministry leaders have crises to take care of and heavy holiday seasons.

Think of when the flow of your business, nonprofit, school, or ministry requires more time than usual. How you respond in those seasons is critical for your life-giving leadership. And before we move on, let me say that long hours should be for a season, not forever. However, leaders who aren't willing to put in the hours when necessary will never become the life-giving leaders we are called to be.

HEAVY LIFTING

When leaders embrace this upgraded call to leadership, they realize they are signing up for heavy lifting. That doesn't necessarily mean physical lifting. For some professions it could be emotional lifting. For pastors it could be spiritual lifting. For counselors it is deep listening and asking thought-provoking questions. In the event business it absolutely means physical lifting. For each event we have pallets and pallets of resources, signage, gifts, journals, and more. All the pallets loaded with goods and supplies have to go somewhere.

Before shipping, the pallets have to be sorted and wrapped, and then they have to be pushed or pulled to their destination. I pride myself on being one of the best pallet wrappers on our staff. I love teaching new staff members how to wrap pallets. Why? Because I love demonstrating the culture we expect from the top down. Does my job description cover pallet wrapping? No. I wrap pallets because we are all in this together.

It's incredibly powerful when leaders who have earned the right to not do heavy lifting (because of their role or title) choose to serve in this way. When your team knows you're willing to push the heaviest pallets along with them, they will follow you. It is one thing to push pallets when you have to, but it's another when you choose to do it.

GETTING DIRTY

Sometimes leadership gets dirty.

My kids have fallen in love with the Spartan races on television. With mud hills, dirty tree logs to climb, and army crawls, these courses have designers who have set the bar for the dirtiest possible races.

I love the postrace interviews with grimy-looking runners. The best part is the smile on their mud-covered faces. They exude joy and happiness even in the midst of pain and trial. There's joy because they pushed through something that's brutally hard. They got dirty and overcame the obstacles. It's what bonds teams.

I'm talking not only about work teams that get physically dirty but also about teams that get metaphorically into the dirt of work. For you it might be choosing to do an internal audit of your organization's finances because you want everything to be above reproach. You have to dig into the financial history and current picture to uncover where work needs to be done.

It could be coaching the team to get to the root of a conflict among staff members. You've got to get dirty before you can move on.

It might be apologizing for certain decisions or actions. Leaders have to own their decisions, attitudes, words, and actions. It often feels as though we get dirty when we admit our mistakes.

This is hard work, but it is an important part of the journey. Mistakes can be like getting wounded. You have to clean out the wounds. It won't get better unless you focus on it. Scars tell the stories of our lives.

Not long ago I was driving my boys to lunch and overheard them tell each other about the best scars they have. They didn't just talk about a scar; they explained how they got it. It's no wonder the scars Jesus carried serve as a reminder of His love and sacrifice for us. Your leadership scars will help tell your story. If you choose to avoid getting dirty, you choose to avoid the scars. Without scars, you'll have a very different story. But when you acknowledge your mistakes, you will be on your way to life-giving leadership.

There's no work-around. You just have to get after it. Life-giving leaders work alongside their team instead of hearing about it from someone else.

How many of you have worked around leaders who have a higher position in the organizational chart and use that to take every shortcut possible? I have watched leaders send emails rather than engage with their hardworking teams. I understand that we must deal with important emails. But not 24-7. Finish the emails and go to work with your team. Get out of your office and walk around the building to see what you can help with.

Clean the dishes in the break room. People will faint when they see you do it.

You can create a life-giving culture by doing the tasks you have earned the right to avoid.

How many parents have stood there with their mouths open when their children cleaned their room without being asked? It is the same feeling when your boss works hard right alongside you.

I do not believe that as followers of Jesus we can just sit on the sidelines of our lives. If you picked up this book, then I trust that you want to lead in such a way that it helps improve the people around you. We have only a short time on this earth, and it would be a shame to miss it by not embracing the call to work hard. We cannot allow the word *lazy* to ever be a label attached to leaders. It's unacceptable and it should always be inaccurate. If we embrace the call to lead well, we will never be seen as lazy.

Working hard is the beginning of the four *S*'s of leadership, because once you embrace this call you can move forward to the always-popular call to sacrifice.

11

A Call to Sacrifice

Life-Giving Leaders
Sacrifice for the Cause

I f you choose to be a leader, it means when everything goes right, you have to give away all the credit. When everything goes wrong, you have to take all the responsibility. That sucks. That's sacrifice."[1]

When Simon Sinek, author of *Leaders Eat Last* and whose "How Great Leaders Inspire Action" TED Talk is still top five of all time, said this, it made a lot of sense to me. It gave me words that captured one of the hardest concepts for leaders to articulate: the sacrifice involved in leadership.

When you have children, you quickly realize what it means to sacrifice. Have you ever had to watch children's television or movies? From Disney's *Frozen* to public television's *Caillou,* sacrifice is required to be a good parent, even when it means trying to enjoy shows with your children. Not always because they are bad (I actually love *Frozen*) but because of the sheer number of times you have to watch!

It's not just television. It's realizing that everything you have, when you get down to it, is for them. Your time. Your money. Your wisdom and knowledge. You frequently put the things you have wanted to do on the back burner. I'm not trying to paint a gray picture; I'm stating the obvious. Being a parent is hard. But as we saw earlier, things of value require sacrifice.

Of course it would be awesome to go skiing in Breckenridge any time you want or go fishing off the coast of Miami or play golf five days a week. But even if these things were possible, I would still give all of it up to have my two boys.

For twenty years I've wanted a Jeep Wrangler. Not a Lamborghini, a Porsche, or a Ferrari. A Jeep Wrangler. I know we're not supposed to think all the time about something we want, but I daydream about driving through the mountains in a Jeep with the top off.

My wife tells me to stop dreaming about Jeeps. She's right, but they pop up in my mind at all the wrong times. And now, every time I reread this section, it takes me a few minutes to stop thinking about a Jeep. One day, when life is a little more settled, I'm pretty sure it will work out for me to have one. However, making sure the members of my family have everything they need will always take priority.

I do just fine in life without a Jeep. As long as I have a vehicle that gets me to and from where I'm going, I'm good. Except not having a Jeep feels like a sacrifice. Don't email me or DM me to mention how shallow this is. I know it already. But I'm being honest. It's a simple example of sacrifice—giving up something you want so other people can have something they need.

Author and pastor Andy Stanley has said many times, "You're saying no for now, but not forever."[2]

Sacrifice should be normal in Christian leadership. Giving yourself to others is part of the plan. Jesus made that abundantly clear. If you want to be first, you choose to be last and you choose to sacrifice for those around you (see Matthew 19:29–30). Leadership requires us to sacrifice things of value.

For many of you, this is an obvious principle. Maybe you've been a believer for a long time and have heard sermons about this. But I'm stating it again because the idea of sacrifice will never be the norm in culture. Leaders who are known to sacrifice to serve others stand out in a good way. People want to be around them because a sacrificial approach to leadership is unique in our me-first society.

Think of a self-sacrificing leader you know. Did you lose respect for that person because that was his or her posture? Now think of leaders who would keep all the perks for themselves and never sacrifice for the people around them. Did your respect for such leaders grow? Giving up your privilege for someone else will change the picture your team and friends have of you.

Sacrifice comes across in a number of ways. Here are a few that come to mind when I think about what you and I likely will have to sacrifice to be life-giving. As you ponder these areas, think about how life-giving this would be if your leader did this for you. It's not difficult to understand why these matter to the people around you as well.

THE POWER OF YOUR TIME

Leading often means sacrificing time, usually at the most inopportune moments. Have you ever gotten ready for bed and then received a text or phone call? Let's say it's not something you consider an emergency but instead involves a friend who might be on the edge of high maintenance. You know if you respond it'll be a long night. You're already reaching for your clothes so you can get dressed and head over to see your friend. Or perhaps it turns into an astoundingly long phone call. These will be hours you'll never get back. Do you pick up the phone or reply to the text message?

Good friends sacrifice for the relationship. When a need arises, they respond with time. Great leaders do the same thing. They understand the power of their time. When your team or peers see you give away your time, they realize they are valuable to you. I want to make sure each of my direct reports understands how important he or she is to me, and the best way I can do that is through my time. I try never to cancel a one-on-one meeting if I can help it. That shows I value my team members.

If you aren't making *consistent* time for your key leaders, their value to you will be questioned. Devoting time to people is a primary way life flows from you to others. Every week, focus on one or two people. It's even better when spending time with them requires going out of your way. Doing this will increase the life flow for that day.

My kids need my time. My wife needs my time. And honestly, *I* need my time. What or who gets your time might well be the clearest indicator of what you value. A sacrifice of time can be five minutes or five hours. Either way, when it's a sacrifice, it's because it forces something else to be on the back burner. Learning to discern when to give time—what's most important at the moment, who needs your time the most, what can be left until later—is a major tool in the life-giving leader's tool kit. It can change everything.

Have leaders ever taken time with you when you knew they didn't have time for it? I met Rick Warren for the first time at a Catalyst One Day event at his church, Saddleback. I had organized and pulled off a number of Catalyst events, but this was the first time I'd been able to spend time with the speakers. It is such a privilege to interact with world-changing leaders such as Rick Warren. I have watched him choose to take ample time with every person he meets, when it is at all possible. When I talked with him, he was generous with his time. He asked to hear a little of my story. He asked about Catalyst. He was genuinely interested in my life.

The entire time I was thinking, *Don't you have somewhere else to be? Isn't there someone more important you need to use your time on?* According to his actions and posture, he was giving his precious time to me, and it made a lasting impact on my leadership.

REJECTING THE LURE OF SELF-INTEREST

US Marine Lieutenant General George Flynn said, "The true cost of the leadership privilege comes at the expense of self-interest."[3] If you wonder why people think leadership is hard, it's because of truths such as this one. When you fully embrace the task of creating a leadership legacy, it will require you to sacrifice your self-interest more frequently than not.

You know how common it is for your plan for the day to get thrown out the window because suddenly you have to put out a fire. Your plans and ideas get put on hold. Many times you're at the office before anybody else gets there, and you're still at the office when everyone leaves. It can be wearing on us physically, mentally, emotionally, and spiritually. The craziest part of it is that, as believers, we can't just halfway embrace the requirement that we give up our self-interest.

Jesus made this one really clear.

> Calling the crowd to join his disciples, he said, "Anyone who intends to come with me has to let me lead. You're not in the driver's seat; *I* am. Don't run from suffering; embrace it. Follow me and I'll show you how. Self-help is no help at all. Self-sacrifice is the way, my way, to saving yourself, your true self. What good would it do to get everything you want and lose you, the real you? What could you ever trade your soul for?" (Mark 8:34–37, MSG)

What? "Self-sacrifice is the way, my way, to saving yourself"? Is there a secular scholar who would ever say such a thing? Who would pledge allegiance to such a crazy proposition? It runs counter to our culture, which is defined by chasing everything you want. And chasing everything now.

Sacrifice is often seen as a bad thing, especially when it's at your expense. Why give money to the homeless when you could be using that money to pay for a vacation to restore your depleted reserves? But Jesus is unyielding on this one. Even when He was preaching the necessity of self-denial, it was at odds with the prevailing conventional wisdom (see, among others, Mark 10:17–23).

Life-giving leaders understand the power of sacrificing today's gratification for a better tomorrow. They know intuitively that it will pay off for others and for themselves in the future. I have a friend who decided to be bold with sacrifice early in his life to have a different life now. From the first day he bought his house, he opted for a fifteen-year mortgage and paid even more principal each month to pay it off as quickly as possible. It was a huge monthly investment early in his career, but sacrificing then to reap the reward of owning his home outright and not having a mortgage during the past decade was worth this sacrifice. The same can be said of leadership. You can choose to play a long-term game (building great culture, hiring well, and so on) rather than just executing today without building a great organization for the long haul.

Why would we do this? Why do the best leaders in the world embrace a radical idea such as this? Why would top leaders, the best and the brightest, give up their own ideas and pursuits to help other people reach theirs?

As followers of Jesus, we understand there are two ways to look at life. We can concentrate on the world we see or on the unseen world. Jesus helped us grasp the spiritual principle at work. He regularly taught the disciples about things unseen—the Upstairs activity—and how that plays out Downstairs in the world. I wonder what these twelve guys felt when Jesus told them to embrace suffering and not run from it.

As we discussed previously, being your truest self means you have signed on for self-sacrifice. As Jesus taught, "Self-sacrifice is the way, my way, to saving yourself, your true self" (Mark 8:35, MSG). The best way to become your truest self and lead from your truest self is through self-sacrifice.

Let me be the first to say out loud that this probably isn't what you were hoping to hear. I don't want to hear it either, most of the time.

Although there is one exception, and that is when I choose others over serving myself first. God moves when you and I choose others. God changes us when we sacrifice for others. I believe God smiles when this happens. I'm not saying there are not going to be times when you choose something for yourself. There are plenty of those times. However, many times when you lead, your leadership can be seen to bring life when you choose another person's interests over your own (see, for example, Philippians 2:3–4).

Think about people you know who choose themselves instead of giving up their agenda to serve other people. Give it some more thought. Picture these people and sense their attitudes and priorities. Doesn't it bother you when you really think about it?

Now think about a few people you know who regularly sacrifice for other people. Do they not exemplify the kind of person you want to be? Are they not incredibly attractive as leaders?

I'm convinced Jesus was onto something in Mark 8. How about you?

Sacrifice makes total sense when you are living Upstairs in the unseen world. Giving up yourself for the people around you pleases the Lord. He can relate to it.

THE MONEY STRUGGLE

Giving up our hard-earned money for the benefit of others isn't easy, even when we're committed to doing it. This is definitely not a principle the world grabs hold of. But we are called to be different from the world. We have Upstairs thinking.

God's economy bears little resemblance to what we see on earth.

Upstairs thinking forces us to realize that we are stewards of God's resources, not investors looking out for our greatest financial return. When you realize you're managing someone else's (God's) money, it makes it easier to give your money away. I'm not talking just about tithing; I'm talking about handing over your money when others need it more.

God calls us to be generous people. It's a better decision in life, and it benefits us as much as it helps other people. Proverbs 11:25 lets us know that "a generous person will prosper; whoever refreshes others will be refreshed" (NIV).

If you have tried this, you know it's true. We love to give gifts, and there's a good reason for it. Something happens in our hearts when we are generous. We change, and we find that money loses its grip on our hearts. Choosing to sacrifice money for others is kryptonite for greed. It crushes the power greed can have over the way we live. The misuse of money can cloud our judgment and hurt relationships as quickly and as effectively as any other factor.

We like to think that when money is tight we are justified in keeping all of it for ourselves. But giving isn't an option. When you look at the generosity shown by Jesus, it's difficult to argue against being generous. For Jesus followers, it should be an unquestioned lifestyle. It shows to whom you have surrendered your life.

It's also a statement of faith. Men and women who give money away as Jesus directs them show that they understand whose money it is. When believers realize we are stewards of God's money, then we can be generous with money. Most days, it'll feel like a sacrifice, but it's no different from other acts of worship. Generosity is an outward display of your belief that God is sovereign.

As a leader I am often called on to make a financial sacrifice for the sake of the team or organization. I wish I could say that every time this has happened I gave generously and with a happy heart. I can't say that, however. It doesn't get easier to give away your money until you understand that just as Jesus gave us our leadership platform, He also gave us financial opportunities.

Leaders, money can capture your heart and drag you away from your God-given commitments. You know that and I know that. Jesus knew that too. Self-sacrifice is a mandate, in part, because it helps to keep us from letting anything less than God ensnare us.

SLEEP AND LOSS OF SLEEP

Leadership causes you to sacrifice some of your sleep. When my boys were born, I couldn't believe that none of my friends had warned me about the effects of sleep deprivation. Both of our boys had acid reflux, so for the first year of their lives they didn't sleep well. I'd go to work after getting only two hours of sleep. I'd be in a meeting and not be able to form a sentence.

You and I know many people who would rather sleep than eat. You might be one of those people. If you are, the idea of sacrificing sleep might be way more difficult than giving up time or giving away money.

If you choose to be a life-giving leader and put others first, losing sleep will often be a part of your leadership journey.

When you take a leadership posture that is focused on others, giving up a little sleep to give people your best is worth it every time. Life-giving leaders get this. We aren't losing sleep because we are anxious about tomorrow but because we care about tomorrow. We want it to be better than yesterday, and that requires preparation and hard work and even, at times, relational confrontation. Let's be the leaders who give freely, getting the world's attention because we present such a contrast to the norm. (We'll wait until the time is right to tell them it's because Jesus gave Himself so freely for us.)

THE CONFLICT CAUSED BY CONFLICT

When you accepted the call to lead well and give life to those around you, you gave up the right to avoid conflict. Jesus spelled out how to keep short accounts and told us to make it a priority: "If you are offering your gift at the altar and there remember that your brother or sister has something against you, leave your gift there in front of the altar. First go and be reconciled to them; then come and offer your gift. Settle matters quickly" (Matthew 5:23–25, NIV).

Why is it that when we are someone's boss or leader, we have a hard time letting go of past conflicts? I can get past conflict with other people when they are friends or family members. Could it be that leaders see staff members as theirs and not God's?

In addition, when conflict arises, it's necessary to act quickly. I have seen staff members take *way* too long to address conflict. (I have struggled with it myself.) I've seen leaders avoid dealing with someone's work ethic or, one of the hardest, a staff member's loss of a fit and good spirit. Then the leader wondered how that person had lost effectiveness and camaraderie with colleagues and passion for the people being served. You might've even heard of the concept of keeping short accounts. That's a powerful principle that's more of a truism now. Keep short accounts. "Do not let the sun go down on your anger" (Ephesians 4:26). In other words, life-giving leaders understand that dealing with anger, frustration, or whatever needs to be swift so it doesn't get a foothold.

Leaders have to address issues when they first occur. That way a leader can prevent the problem from growing into something bigger and more damaging. It's much harder to deal with a problem that has gotten out of hand. If we leaders are willing to push through the awkwardness of the confrontation, we will see massive breakthroughs.

Best-selling Christian author Max Lucado wrote, "Conflict is inevitable, but combat is optional."[4]

When we are trying to bring life and abundance to a monochrome world, this could be one of the greatest splashes of vibrancy possible. Confrontation is awkward and difficult. I don't know anyone who would deny it. Confrontation requires thought and putting yourself out there. But dealing with a small issue now instead of allowing it to grow changes the game in organizations. It also changes your relationship with your leaders.

You will do a far better job of dealing with conflict if you have previously invested heavily in relational capital. As leadership expert John Maxwell wrote, "People don't care how much you know until they know how much you care."[5] It's absolutely true when it comes to conflict. When you deal with conflict but have no relational capital, it's virtually impossible for things to go well. However, if you confront someone in whom you have made relational investments, chances are good that you will bring life through your conversation. If people can see that a leader really cares about them, the amount of grace shown in these situations can be incredible.

I'm not saying that if you do this it will always go well. But I *will* guarantee that if you don't care for people before you attempt to deal with conflict, it will be a difficult mountain to overcome. Always.

You never know where leaders stand in their ability to handle conflict. That's why our growth and willingness to have hard conversations force life to flow in the right direction. We can't rely on the maturity of staff members to make up for our lack of preparation and care.

Because it matters, all of this requires sacrifice. And you know it's worth it. People follow leaders who deal with conflict swiftly, cautiously, and with care.

HOW ABOUT YOU?

Life flows through sacrifice. You have to make a sacrifice now to receive the fruit later. Life-giving leaders accept the call to sacrifice as a better way to lead. I will follow leaders who sacrifice their own interest, sleep, time, and comfort to pour into me. All day, every day.

What is one thing you can do in the next seven days to sacrifice for someone else? Maybe family, friends, coworkers, or even someone you just met? I challenge you to take five minutes and pray that God would shed light on areas in which He is leading you to make a sacrifice. Not for the sake of sacrifice alone but because of what it does in and around you.

It doesn't stop here, however. Life-giving leaders don't just sweat and sacrifice for the leaders around them; life-giving leaders change their circle of influence by living out the next call.

12

A Call to Surrender

Life-Giving Leaders
Surrender to God's Will

I'm not sure there is another principle in this book that has as many historical illustrations. So many past and present leaders have embodied surrender that I feel I'm doing an injustice to each one by pairing them with other leaders. One of the greatest examples of surrender is Martin Luther King Jr. Not only was he committed to racial equality, but he had surrendered to getting there without relying on violence. Throughout thirteen years of leadership aimed at racial equality, he stayed committed to nonviolent protest even when he and fellow demonstrators and leaders were assaulted. You can't win the Nobel Peace Prize at the age of thirty-five unless you've surrendered to something bigger than your own life.

King surrendered to the Lord's call by standing up for what's right *and* doing so in the manner he was convicted to. He might be one of the greatest examples in history of a life-giving leader. His legacy and work continue to bring life to people. He knew his unique place in the story and he accepted it. It required surrendering to something bigger than he ever thought.

As we learn about life-giving leadership, I trust you have seen that leadership that gives life to others correlates with the following five ideas.

First, how God designed you. You lead best when you lead from your true self.

Second, you respond to the call to sweat. You can't give life as a leader unless you work much harder than most people alive today.

Third, you answer the call to sacrifice. The best leaders know that none of this is about them; it's about the people they lead.

Fourth, life-giving leaders surrender to God's will. We could never figure all this out on our own. We have to be following a guide, which for us is the will of God.

If you hold on to things with a white-knuckle grip, life flow will move in only one direction: toward you. This is true even if what you're holding on to is a good thing, such as dreams, family, love, or work. Even good things have to be released. When your fists are clenched, trying to hold on to something, they aren't open to receive.

Jesus often talked about the cost of following Him: "Whoever wants to be my disciple must deny themselves and take up their cross and follow me" (Mark 8:34, NIV). In the gospel of Matthew, Jesus said, "Follow me, and let the dead bury their own dead" (Matthew 8:22, NIV). He wasn't being a jerk or coldhearted. I believe Jesus was living out an Upstairs narrative rather than a Downstairs one.

UPSTAIRS AND DOWNSTAIRS

Dionne van Zyl, CEO and chairman of the board at Catalyst, shared an amazing insight that has become a beautiful guide for me. He drew some parallels between *Downton Abbey* and how God operates.

On the PBS series *Downton Abbey* (probably my wife's favorite show), you see a narrative take shape. The workers at the huge family estate live and work downstairs. The Crawleys, who own the house (in real life it's a castle), live upstairs. Every decision made upstairs sends the downstairs community to work. For example, if Lord Grantham (Robert Crawley, head of the family) decides to go hunting, chaos ensues downstairs to prepare for the hunt and ensure it goes smoothly.

It would be similar to a work environment in which you are handed decisions from the executive wing and never understand where the decision came from or why. That and *Downton Abbey* are examples of earthbound Upstairs decision-making. But when God is the decision maker, the process, purpose, and results differ greatly.

On the show (now off the air), some of the drama took place upstairs. But most of the drama on the television screen happened downstairs when the workers would question why certain decisions were being made. An announcement of a new upstairs decision could unleash downstairs frustration because almost any decision interrupted and redirected downstairs work.

Why was this analogy so meaningful to me? Because the drama in our lives takes place Downstairs, through circumstances and developments having to do with earthly plans and concerns. It's even worse when we don't have all the facts, but when do we really ever have all the facts? These are the circumstances when we speculate on why something happens. We think we have better information and a clearer point of view, so we question God, the decision maker.

Have you ever felt that way when God interrupts your short-range or long-range plans with something else He wants you to focus on? Yeah, me neither. Just asking for a friend.

Back to the *Downton Abbey* illustration: Throughout the show, viewers witnessed an astounding amount of speculation about what Lord Grantham was thinking. The downstairs workers would bicker constantly about the decisions. They would often second-guess Robert Crawley's thinking.

Many times throughout the series, you could tell what the staff thought about the upstairs decisions just by looking at their body language. It was perfect, because it was us. It was you, and it was me.

Have you ever watched God do something and then just like that you were thinking, *Hmm, not what I would do, but God's the boss*? Or maybe you thought, *Why isn't God answering this the way I want Him to? I let Him know all the facts and the reasons why my plan is better.* Whatever the case may be, we often find ourselves confused because the heavenly response differs from our earthly thinking.

Sidenote: Have you noticed that your parents' and grandparents' generations talked and dreamed of heaven more than we do? Everything will make sense when we are in heaven, right? Heaven is a dream destination. Clarity, love, peace. It's all there. Why have we lost the passion for heaven? Longing to see heaven is similar to the Upstairs narrative. When we long for heaven to come down, I argue that it's usually because order reigns in heaven. We long for order and peace. God's plan makes sense when seen with a heavenly perspective. Upstairs thinking is how we can live in step with heaven before we get there.

Back to the *Downton Abbey* illustration: Is it crazy to think that the upstairs narrative might reveal a more comprehensive understanding of what needs to happen downstairs? Could it be that Lord Grantham has more information and experience than the people who serve downstairs?

Here's the beauty of this incredible insight that my friend shared. Not only are we, as followers of Jesus, invited to visit Upstairs from time to time, but we are also invited to *live* Upstairs. We are heirs, sons and daughters. Heirs don't live downstairs; they live upstairs. They dine upstairs. They learn the ways of the lord of the house. They make upstairs decisions that lead to work getting done downstairs. Life-giving leaders have adopted an Upstairs point of view, and it helps frame their decision-making with proper perspective.

Which way do you think life will flow in the Upstairs/Downstairs narrative? It flows from Upstairs to Downstairs. When we receive from God, we can give to others. When we sit with God Upstairs, we understand how to spread life Downstairs.

CLARITY PAVES THE WAY FOR SURRENDER

I became a believer when I was in high school. It wasn't long afterward that people started asking if I wanted to go into full-time Christian ministry. Maybe they were asking because of my natural relational skills or my lack of fear in front of people. I wasn't able to answer yes or no, but I did feel immense clarity regarding one thing. I didn't fully understand why, but I didn't want to override God's plan for me.

Somehow, my spirit understood something I hadn't put into words. There was an Upstairs narrative, a heavenly plan, and my spirit sensed that. I wanted to be aligned with the Lord's ideas because somehow I knew they are always better. Always.

The Upstairs story became clear one night in 1996. I was a sophomore at the University of Georgia. We were having a worship service at the Wesley Foundation, which is the campus ministry I attended. Every Wednesday night we gathered and pursued the Lord together.

On this night, the stirring of my heart was an answer to the question of my calling. I decided during the prayer time after the message that I would do some serious Jacob-style wrestling with the Lord. (The good news is that no hips were injured in this story.)

That's when I entered the Upstairs narrative and stood in God's presence for the first time. I had encountered God before, but not like this. I had placed my trust in Him years before, but this was different. I was invited to visit Upstairs.

As soon as my knees hit the altar (we had old-school kneeling benches), I was no longer living Downstairs. I was invited Upstairs. What seemed like five minutes (though I never wanted it to end) was actually an hour.

When you get a taste of Upstairs, you crave it forever. Upstairs is different. It's calm. It's peaceful. It's devoid of chaos. Clarity and excitement rule. Passion and love are ever-present. God is there.

Listen, leaders. Surrender is easy when you have experienced God like that. A Father who invites you not only to visit Upstairs but to live there gains your trust. We will be asked to work Downstairs until God calls us home. However, working Downstairs with an Upstairs posture changes everything. When our day-to-day lives follow Upstairs thinking, surrender is a natural response because we know that something different is at play. Life has new layers to it. Giving ourselves to something bigger than our plans becomes a natural response. Listen to how Paul addressed the work we do Downstairs: "Let every detail in your lives—words, actions, whatever—be done in the name of the Master, Jesus, thanking God the Father every step of the way" (Colossians 3:17, MSG).

For me, our discussion of surrender is much more a leadership posture and understanding than a practical day-to-day leadership strategy. When we embrace a call to surrender, priority and posture become the secret sauce for the Lord's work in our lives and our leadership.

Priority

Choosing what to prioritize serves as one of the most important elements of having a full life. Prioritizing is central to being a life-giving leader. Prioritizing the Lord is crucial to this conversation.

As I mentioned earlier, my wife and I could not be more grateful for our two boys and the men they are becoming. When our older son was born, I started to understand the importance of priorities. My ten years of working at North Point Ministries under Andy Stanley's consistent leadership truly framed my perspective on prioritizing family over work. I always understood that I could delegate tasks at work to someone at work, but I could never delegate things at home to anyone else. And you don't want to. I know I don't want to. That message was *massive* for me as I began the work of prioritizing my family. I had already established my wife and our marriage as my top priority. Now I was adding another layer: my kids. (Stanley's book *When Work and Family Collide* is a great addition for this concept.[1])

I had to travel and be away from home some nights. I was still in a position that required I work weekends and put in long days. However, I understood that those would be exceptions, not the rule. The long days, nights, and weekends had to be planned in advance; they couldn't be the normal mode of operation. And I had to lead my team that way too. I needed to model recovery and priority and allow staff members the same opportunity.

I heard many experts talk about a personal or family budget in these terms: either you can decide where the money goes or it will decide for you.

The same thing applies when prioritizing the Lord's movement and plan for your life. Either you prioritize His place in your life and leadership or God will have to move in different ways. It's a question of whether or not there are things in your life that are hindering the flow of life from God to others through you. Ego, pride, selfish ambition, and so on. Wrong priorities cut off the flow of life.

Here are ideas on how to prioritize and surrender daily to God's plan through your leadership.

- Start your day with a quick prayer asking God what He has in store for your day.
- Prioritize the needs and interests of another person over your plans and agenda. I believe the Lord finds pleasure in that. God's plan always involves people.

- Spend time alone and think through your priorities for the day. Family, work, yourself. Then ask the Lord what He wants to do in each of those areas. Are His priorities lining up with yours? This one is hard, and I wouldn't recommend doing it more than once or twice a year. Ask your trusted friends, whom you've given permission to speak into your life, to take a glance at your leadership and see where they notice you're placing your priorities. It's a painful exercise but incredibly valuable. (Note: If you haven't given anyone permission to speak into your life, take care of that now.)

Legendary leadership guru and thought leader Jim Collins has written at length about having a personal board of directors. In 1996 he wrote,

> I mean a *personal* board of directors composed of . . . people you deeply respect and would not want to let down. A group like a set of tribal elders that you turn to for guidance at times of ethical dilemma, life transitions, and difficult choices, people who embody the core values and standards you aspire to live up to.[2]

Posture

The second key to surrender, after priority, is posture. Posture can serve you and your leadership well across all four of these key principles of leadership.

At Catalyst, we have a consistent prayer. I'm not sure there has been a more important prayer in the life of our team. It is this: "God, move through us and not in spite of us."

It's all about posture. Place yourself in God's path so He will move through you and won't have to go around you. I want that for myself, and I want that for my team.

I recently heard speaker, consultant, and leader Graham Cooke say that Jesus said to seek first the kingdom and *He* will build the church.[3] We are not the ones who build the church. We must surrender and have a correct posture in regard to God's position and plan. We often work for God but fail to spend time with Him. We may be building things for Him without knowing if that's even what He desires.

Surrendering to God requires time with Him. The best posture for life-giving leaders is to be on our knees and sometimes our faces in worship and prayer. Surrender is birthed in quiet places with the Lord. This is what the call to surrender is all about. Getting the right perspective comes from being in the right posture. A kingdom posture. A place of hearing and receiving before doing, which is a place of worship.

Maintaining a posture of worship could be the absolute best leadership advice any of us could hear. When we place ourselves in a posture of worship, God places Himself in the right place in our lives. It's Upstairs living versus Downstairs doing.

A posture of surrender could be the thing that changes your outcomes more than any other factor. We all have areas of our lives and leadership that need to be jump-started, cut out, or revised. What are the odds that surrendering to God in a posture of worship could be the place He wants you to reach? What if God has chosen not to reveal your breakthrough until He breaks through to you?

Let me share a couple of practical posture ideas.

- At the beginning of the day, limit what enters your mind and heart. I won't listen to anything but worship music until nine or ten in the morning. I want my heart and mind to surrender to light, grace, and God. Worship helps me do that.
- Designate a spot for worship—perhaps a chair, a bench, or a walking path. Once you have identified somewhere, meet with God there. Your spot will contribute to the proper posture when you make it a consistent place to meet with God.
- Enter your office, church, or building every day with your palms up. Repeat a simple prayer telling the Lord that you will try to steward His name well.

Life-giving leaders have a proper priority and posture, and people see it. Teams want to follow leaders who are surrendered to something bigger than themselves. Not only do we represent ourselves, but we also represent Jesus to the world. We do not belong to ourselves. We were bought with a price, so we belong to God. Everything we do is for Him. Our faith is a live-it-out-daily faith.

I was telling a friend about wanting to surrender to God so He could use me. My friend asked about possible comparisons to things I use. I thought of tools, equipment, a laptop, other aids to getting work done.

But I didn't think of people. People are not tools to use to advance our own work on earth. I was overwhelmed by the beauty of that thought. God teaches us how to live, but He does not use us in a utilitarian way. Instead, He chooses to work alongside us.

There is no substitute for understanding God's love for us. It changes our perspective again and again. He's with us while we try to lead well, and He's with us when we struggle. He speaks to us as we learn, and He moves around us to reveal His glory.

God doesn't want to use us; He wants to partner with us for His glory.

Our surrender to God is a surrender to a relationship with our heavenly Father. When we choose to prioritize and posture our lives properly, we allow the relationship to grow and move forward. Then we will find ourselves in the middle of what God is doing in our leadership.

GOD HAS GOT THIS

Pastor and prayer warrior Tom Tanner (and my mentor in college) is one of the leaders who has had the greatest impact on my life and leadership. My faith grew immensely during my years at the University of Georgia, and much of that I credit to Tom's leadership.

The community at the Wesley Foundation has forever marked me, and I believe the work of this ministry has sent many men and women into full-time vocational ministry. Tom has talked about what it was like to be new in the ministry role at Wesley. He mentioned that he felt completely overwhelmed by the task at hand. He took the job out of surrender to God's plan, and he was both excited and fearful.

A couple of days before the school year kicked off, he was sitting outside the ministry center, experiencing the same crazy feeling many of us have felt. He was nervous. He might well have wondered if God had chosen the right leader for the ministry at the Wesley Foundation.

While he was telling me this story, I could see a shine in his eyes as he remembered the moment God met with him. In that moment, life flowed from the Lord to Tom's heart and ultimately to the thousands of students he influenced.

He said he prayed out loud, *God, I cannot do this.* God responded to him with what felt like an audible voice: *I've got this!*

It wouldn't make sense to surrender to a being or a movement or an idea that can let you down. If God were ever to let any of us down, we would be the first. We serve a sovereign, holy, life-giving God, and He is not in the business of being unfaithful. He's faithful and just. He's good. Choosing to surrender to God is the right decision, and you will never regret it.

Can you remember the last time you spent significant time with the Lord in prayer and worship? Is there a canyon between you and the Lord that needs to be crossed before you can move on to the next chapter? What if you were to take thirty minutes right now to posture yourself before the Lord and ask for innovation from heaven for a situation you need help with? Do you need to be reminded by your heavenly Father that He is with you as you attempt to honor Him and others in your leadership?

God has got this. For you and for me. For your team. For your family. We just have to surrender to our relationship with Him.

13

A Call to Serve

Life-Giving Leaders Serve Others

Please, Lord, help me get one more."[1] That was the prayer of Private First Class Desmond Doss as he served as a medic in World War II. The hero of the movie *Hacksaw Ridge* embodied the idea of serving.

Doss grew up in Lynchburg, Virginia. He had a turbulent upbringing and an alcoholic father, yet his mother was a strong woman of God. The scriptural grounding that his mother gave him would be the backbone of his life story.

The craziest part of his role in the Battle of Okinawa in 1945 was that Doss never fired a weapon. It was one of the war's bloodiest battles, with casualties projected at more than 160,000 Japanese and American troops. The Allies wanted to secure the island as a base of operations, but the Japanese used every measure, including civilians dressed as soldiers, to defend it. Hacksaw Ridge presented some of the most difficult terrain for an invading force to cover.

And that's where Doss became the war hero who never fired a round. He was surrendered fully to the idea that "while everybody else is taking life, I'm going to be saving it."[2] Doss became a target for ridicule when he first enlisted. However, he stayed true to his convictions and his desire to serve. It was his faith in God that compelled him to lay down his life for those around him. He called himself a conscientious cooperator. He said he chose to go to war because he was eager to wear the uniform, salute the American flag, and give everything he had to serve his country. He made the choice to serve, and in doing so he rescued some seventy-five Allied soldiers while under heavy fire. That's what life-giving leaders choose.

I can't imagine going to war with a conviction that I knew would prevent me from ever firing a weapon in battle. But Doss never lacked courage. In his heroic rescue operation, he created special knots to use in lowering men from the high ground that was being bombarded. He was able to get them down to where they received medical help, all the while avoiding the enemy.

What an incredible story of embracing a call to serve. He was the first conscientious objector to win the congressional Medal of Honor, awarded him by President Harry S. Truman on October 12, 1945.[3] Desmond Doss was so driven to serve that he worked out a way to enter battle as a Christian who was convinced that God opposes war. Men returned home alive after the war because Doss risked his life, time and time again, to pull them off the battlefield to safety.

Serving is a choice that anyone can make. But for believers in Jesus, serving is not optional. Think of men and women who gave up lives to serve those around them. Mother Teresa, Nelson Mandela, maybe a neighbor, or your mom and dad. My grandfather comes to mind when I think of servants. He was a fire chief in Atlanta and served in the Korean War. If a need presented itself, he was ready to serve.

There is something compelling and authentic about leaders who put their personal interests and goals aside to focus on helping someone else. Life-giving leaders understand that no matter how far up the ladder they go in an organization, they will always strive to serve the people on their team.

I didn't think up this principle. Jesus made this one really clear.

JESUS'S WAY IS A CLEAR CONTRAST

The teachings found in Matthew 20 present a clear contrast between how most of the world operates and how Christians should be different. It shouldn't come as a surprise that the teachings are those of Jesus, who was (and will always be) the greatest servant of all time.

Jesus had been teaching on a variety of subjects, and the disciples had shown they didn't comprehend all that He was saying. We read in Matthew 19 that Jesus rebuked the disciples for not letting some children come to Him. I can see the disciples' side of it. Jesus was busy and they were trying to protect His time.

But for Jesus, the Upstairs narrative was what mattered. That narrative prioritizes people.

Then in Matthew 20 we read a story Jesus told about workers in a vineyard. They each received the same amount of money in exchange for working unequal lengths of time. Some of the men felt this system was unfair.

Put yourself in the shoes of the people who had worked the longest hours and were paid the same as the ones who started much later. You know it would bother you. It would bother me.

While the disciples were trying to recover from this difficult teaching, another crazy thing happened. The mother of James and John asked Jesus if her sons could sit at His right and at His left. It's widely believed that James and John wanted to occupy positions of honor and they asked their mom to ask Jesus about it.

Excuse me? What? Are you telling me that two grown men who gave up their lives to serve Jesus still struggled with the need for respect?

Of course, being a follower of Jesus never makes us less human, and it doesn't seal us off from petty human concerns. Choosing to be life-giving leaders and embrace a call to serve will never completely take away our desire to be known. The question becomes, What do you want to be known for?

This is where we pick up our teaching. Jesus needed to settle things down. Can you imagine the tension in the room? Think about it: two of the disciples made it known they wanted to be the favorites and occupy places of honor next to Jesus. Haven't you wanted that before? And haven't you been around leaders who pursued the place of honor in their organizations?

It's not wrong to want to grow and gain influence. Jesus, however, had a different posture toward gaining influence. This is one of the few times in Scripture where I'm aware that Jesus made a massive shift in our thinking. There's no way around His teaching. He was crystal clear: "It's not going to be that way with you" (Matthew 20:26, MSG).

The New International Version makes it even clearer: "Not so with you." It's rare that I read the Scriptures and find a truth this clear. Jesus stated that the world leads like this, but we don't. "You know that the rulers of the Gentiles lord it over them, and their high officials exercise authority over them. *Not so with you*" (Matthew 20:25–26, NIV). The expression "lord it over them" is telling. There is only one Lord, and we know that Jesus is Lord. It's as if leaders who don't follow Jesus want to use their position to act like lords. If you have put your faith in Jesus, you don't have this option. Christians *must* act in a manner that runs counter to the prevailing culture. It's not just a good idea; Jesus gave us a mandate.

Before you read the next part, take a second to return to Upstairs thinking. Do you think perhaps that this is one of the times when our Upstairs narrative changes our Downstairs behavior?

Upside-Down Greatness

The passage continues: "Whoever wants to be great must become a servant. . . . That is what the Son of Man has done: He came to serve, not be served—and then to give away his life in exchange for the many who are held hostage" (Matthew 20:26–28, MSG).

This is not an abstract teaching. Jesus was clear. If you want to be great, serve. Choosing to serve others shows a commitment to the kingdom story. Life-giving leaders choose this commitment. They live to serve.

Quick sidenote: I believe that whether you choose to serve because of faith or you choose to serve because it's a good leadership posture, this is one of the greatest leadership qualities a person can be known for. Servant leaders always have followers.

Do you want to know why I'm so passionate about this passage? Have you ever read a book by someone you know and felt a disconnect? Or have you ever been led by a person who teaches one thing and does something else? When Jesus taught this principle, there was no question on whether He consistently lived it out. As a matter of fact, in Matthew 20, He had just predicted His death and resurrection for the third time. Jesus was the greatest servant the world has seen—to the point of giving up His life for those around Him. That's life-giving leadership. Literally.

Who among us will be asked to sacrifice ourselves for others to the point of death? Perhaps none of us will. However, every day we have a choice to give life to others by serving them. We frequently see leaders resist serving. They'd rather be served. They feel they have paid their dues and earned the right to not have to serve in this way or that.

For some it's an issue of time management. At a top leader's pay grade, it's not financially sustainable for the CEO to leave his office to empty the dishwasher in the break room. We can make fun of James and John for having their mom ask Jesus to give them favorable treatment. We can criticize their egos and self-centered attitudes. However, I have a feeling we've all been there before. Many times, choosing to serve isn't anyone's first impulse, but I would argue it's the right one.

What Does Serving as a Leader Look Like?

There are so many practical ways to think about serving. For this chapter I have three thoughts regarding service as a leader.

Putting Others First

Scripture is clear about the importance of putting other people first. Paul didn't equivocate on this requirement: "Love one another with brotherly affection. Outdo one another in showing honor" (Romans 12:10). My wife and I have always believed that submitting to each other should be a contest of who can serve the other the most. Mutual submission in marriage or in friendship should be characterized by service to each other by putting the other person first.

Here's the crazy thing, leaders: when the leader of the organization chooses to put the team first, everyone wins.

I know this mandate violates almost everything we think of as workable, practical, and sensible in the workplace. There is just no way you can always put everyone else first. How would you get anything done? It might sound selfish, but sometimes you have to take care of yourself first.

I don't disagree. As a matter of fact, if you don't take care of yourself, you will have no ability to serve others. Healthy leaders can give the most when they do a good job of taking care of themselves.

Serving others is more about posture than position. It's about choosing to value others by doing things to serve them. Today it might be getting coffee for your team. Or it could be that you need to take someone to lunch and hear what's going on in his or her world. Perhaps someone at work needs help to learn a new skill, a skill you have already mastered.

When did you last leave your office with the purpose of figuring out a way to serve those around you? I have a feeling that if you ask the Lord, He will give you some insight on where to serve.

The Platinum Rule

Over a decade ago, I was introduced to a personality assessment called RightPath. It has become my go-to resource when it comes to personality assessments.

As children we are taught to follow the Golden Rule: "Do unto others as you would want them to do unto you." It's a good rule to live by. Even if we were to take this rule to heart and stop there, we'd make great progress as a culture.

However, let me tell you about a valuable idea known as the Platinum Rule. RightPath refers to doing unto others as they would want done unto them. In other words, learn your people and serve them in the ways that would mean the most to them.

Let's say one of your staff members is having a birthday today. I think the default for celebration is surprise and attention. If we make a big deal about you and your birthday in front of everyone, it means we love you. But does it mean that to everyone?

If the birthday person is an extrovert, being made the center of attention absolutely conveys the message that he or she is loved by the staff. But if the birthday person is introverted, the staff's bringing cupcakes and singing "Happy Birthday" will be appreciated, but the person still might struggle with feeling valued. What would it look like if you understood each of your team members enough to be able to celebrate them best? If you celebrated introverted team members in a style that matched their wiring, how much more valued would they feel?

If you choose to be a life-giving leader, then you're going to choose to take the extra step. Even something as simple as celebrating someone's birthday in a way that values him or her can be a game changer for your organization and your team members. Why not take another opportunity to study your team, member by member, to learn how to lead each of them best? Some of your leaders need to be asked what they are thinking, because they will usually allow extroverts to take over meetings. Often you need to let the people who are high on a daring scale push you to take some risk, and occasionally you have to pull them back. Learning this uniqueness with the people around you helps you navigate the daily workflow.

Removing Frustration

Have you ever begun something when you had a bad attitude and then, as time went on, you forgot what you had been mad about? This happens in my marriage. My wife will ask me to do something such as fold the laundry or take out the trash, and my response is often less than perfect. And yet something happens to my heart when I serve my wife in these ways.

It is difficult to stay frustrated with people when you choose to serve them. I'm not saying you're going to be a perfect human being when you serve someone. I'm saying that something happens to your heart, even when you start out frustrated, if you choose to put someone else first.

Try it and see what happens.

After twenty-five years spent following Jesus, I've learned that when you submit to the principles of Scripture, some things happen that you can't explain. Many people would say something supernatural happens in your heart, soul, and relationships when they are placed into God's hands. I believe that what Jesus taught in Matthew 20 shows the God-centered behavior of men and women who are devoted to His plan.

It's hard to argue against the truth that God changes you when you serve. Serving is in Jesus's DNA and, therefore, should be in the DNA of every person who follows Him. We can't apply this principle only to our lives outside the office. When you carry this into the workplace, and even more so in your leadership opportunities, it is a game changer. Would you want to work for someone who serves others? If your answer is yes, then why aren't you that person?

Let's look again at the four S's:

- A call to sweat
- A call to sacrifice
- A call to surrender
- A call to serve

This is what life-giving leadership is made of. The best leaders allow life to flow from them by committing to these concepts.

What if we show the world what it looks like to use our leadership and our influence for something bigger than ourselves? Imagine your boss doing that. Imagine your spouse or significant other doing that. Imagine your sister or brother doing that. Imagine yourself doing that.

The world should wonder how we lead so well, why we sacrifice for others, why we work so hard, and to whom we have surrendered our lives.

How we lead affects people's faith, and poor leadership can destroy it. Let's be different.

Jesus modeled all four of these calls: sweating, sacrificing, surrendering, and serving.

- Jesus worked and sweated to teach and care for others.
- Jesus sacrificed everything, including His life, for us.
- Jesus lived fully surrendered.
- Jesus chose to always serve first.

Success at the Four S's

About two years ago our sons attended Vacation Bible School at a nearby church. This was the second or third time they were part of a VBS week. From what I could tell, the week was going great. The boys always spoke highly of the groups and the activities.

But on a Thursday afternoon, the day VBS was over for the week, my wife picked up the boys and noticed something different about our older son. He had a glow about him. She stopped the car in the parking lot and asked him what was going on. He replied with a big grin. "Mommy, I accepted Jesus into my heart today!"

If you've ever seen this happen in a person's life, you know exactly the glow I'm talking about. It still makes me tear up to think about the story because that's the moment our faith became his faith.

Here's the crazy part of this story: my boys have always attended kids groups and church. (They still think they can go into the greenroom to get doughnuts, and I haven't worked at that church in five years!) They have grown up hearing worship and knowing about Jesus. And yet it was at a Vacation Bible School at a church we don't attend, with a group of people we've never met, where his salvation story began. At VBS he stepped from darkness into light and from death into life.

Leaders, if I could, I would go to each person who had any part in VBS that week and say, "Thank you!" Thank you for choosing to work hard and sweat in the middle of the summer in Georgia. Thank you for sacrificing your vacation time and time with your family. Thank you for surrendering to the most life-giving Source on the planet. Thank you for serving children you had never met before.

When people buy in and embrace a lifestyle characterized by these four calls—to sweat, to sacrifice, to surrender, and to serve—lives are changed. Life flows. Grace flows. And my son finds Jesus. Other people find Jesus.

Life-giving leaders allow these four characteristics to be the litmus test for how they're doing. This is life-altering leadership. Which of the four *S*'s do you need to lean into this week? Is there one you have been resisting? Where does the Lord want to upgrade your leadership so you can let the life that flows from you change those around you?

Part 4

How Life-Giving Leaders Change Organizations

Have you ever walked into an organization, church, or business and felt life oozing from the walls? Apple does it. Nike does it. Nordstrom does it. The Ritz-Carlton does it.

The culture they create allows their leaders to operate at their best. There's an energy in those organizations that is felt by staff and customers alike. They are doing something that brings life to those within the organization.

Let me state the obvious: life that enriches people in these organizations is the life and joy you can have from relationships and a fulfilling workplace. The Jesus part enters when Christians lead in a life-giving way. Many of you are not in Christian organizations such as a church, mission, or Christian school. But we should all strive to create or be part of life-giving cultures and serve those who are entrusted to us. Without leaders who choose to be about something bigger than themselves, it's difficult to create that kind of culture. They have to believe in the mission and the people who will help them reach it.

Organizations are always better when they have life-giving leaders. It's that simple. I will take a leader who is fighting to be life-giving over the candidates with the most impressive pedigrees but who aren't working to improve their leadership. You can tell the difference. What kind of questions do they ask? What are their hopes and dreams for their career? Do they ask about leadership development?

If you hire and develop leaders who are life-giving, they will help you transform your team and organization. I'm not saying they don't need the right skills to couple with how they lead, because they absolutely do. But they will have the intangibles.

Let's take a practical look at how life-giving leadership can make a huge impact on our organizations.

14

The Wizard of Oz

Life-Giving Leaders Create Vibrant Organizations

I love *The Wizard of Oz* for so many reasons. Each character needs something to make them who they want to be. There is the tension of people figuring out who they are and what they need to become a better version of themselves. Then there's the wizard acting like something he's not. Such a great story.

My favorite scene is when Dorothy and Toto land in Oz for the first time. What a beautiful scene. Dorothy has just gone through what was likely the most traumatic experience of her life—lifted and spun around by a tornado of epic proportions. Something so massive, so out of control, so terrifying. It was a natural disaster that only a few survive. And worse, it is depicted in black and white!

I love the work of Ansel Adams as much as the next guy, but black and white? Monochrome? Gray? Who wants to live in a monochrome world? Who wants to be known for a lack of vibrant color?

I don't care if Dorothy and Toto started out in a monochrome world. They were transported through the air in a house, which landed with a bang. The girl and the dog couldn't help but be curious as to what was outside. Behind the door was a different world—a new world. Color. Vibrancy. Beauty. Abundance. Emotion. Life. Hope!

Dorothy experienced a life-altering moment. She was given a new perspective. Curiosity and excitement must have flooded her heart. Even more, the audience experienced something for the first time in the history of film: Technicolor. What had been black and white, dull and void of color, underwent one of the most vibrant and emotional metamorphoses ever seen on film.[1]

Life-giving leaders create this metamorphic change in bland organizations. They can bring life to dead places. The best leaders can ignite teams to flourish as never before. They can expect Technicolor moments, the moments when leaders change the climate of the room. Many times an organization's color can change immediately. Sometimes it requires little adjustments over time. Either way, it changes.

We live in an age in which companies, organizations, and even churches feel bland. In the midst of an epidemic of poor leadership, people are dying for someone to bring life back into their homes and workplaces. It could be as simple as taking your team bowling for a couple of hours. Fun activities and surprises can serve as a catalyst for productivity. Taking time out of a busy work schedule can improve the team's performance. When was the last time you took your key leaders off-site just to enjoy some time hanging out? When you make time for normal conversation, you see that everyone is a person trying to work out her or his leadership journey.

Life-giving leaders attract other great leaders because life is flowing and the leaders bring excitement to their places of work or influence. Great leaders follow the leadership of organizations that seem to be filled with color and hope. You can be selling the most uninspiring widget, but if your

company learns the art of life-giving leadership, watch the profits rise. Watch staff satisfaction skyrocket. Watch the church grow. Watch the colors change.

Author and leadership consultant Patrick Lencioni is one of my favorite writers of the past decade. The way he simply explains leadership and the power of healthy, color-filled organizations is powerful. In his book *The Advantage,* we find an abundance of great thoughts on this subject. He wrote, "An organization has *integrity*—is healthy—when it is whole, consistent, and complete, that is, when its management, operations, strategy, and culture fit together and make sense."[2]

PEOPLE COUNT

Healthy, life-giving leaders create healthy, life-giving organizations. It's simple to say but incredibly hard to do. That's why so many businesses ignore this. They don't take the time to gain the advantage. They make short-term decisions to deal with the low-hanging fruit and fail to invest deeply in building a thriving, powerful culture. People crave that kind of strong culture and they thrive in it. Leaders become the leaders God is making them to be when they are empowered to learn and equipped to lead.

Your life-giving leadership can bring color to monochrome organizations. Leaders who choose to lead well let life flow. They are "leaders worth following."[3] I want to be a leader who is worth following. The key word in there is *worth*.

Worth has been defined as "the value equivalent to that of someone or something under consideration; the level at which someone or something deserves to be valued or rated."[4]

Deserving of value. Following a leader not just because of his or her position or rank but because this is leadership that deserves value. If you

seek to be that type of leader, know that it does not come without a hand-some price tag. It requires your days. Your time. Your sacrifice. Your sleep-less nights. Your ego. Your title. Even your success, at times.

Life-giving leaders redefine success. What is success if you leave a wake of bodies behind you, staff members who will never talk to you again?

Contrast that with people who work for life-giving leaders. They've never regretted choosing to follow a leader who works at investing in peo-ple. People over profit. People over results. People over a title.

I want to change the world while I'm changing someone else's world. I want the lives of people around me to be changed because of me. I want to have a legacy of raising people up and helping them reach their full potential. People flourishing because they were led well. I want the leaders around me to grow closer to their heavenly Father.

RED UMBRELLA

Back in the 1980s and 1990s, a series of posters illustrated this idea. The posters were black-and-white photographs of smiling or playing children. Uniquely, within the black-and-white photo, one child, along with what-ever he or she was holding or touching, was in color. Usually a splash of red.

When you look at these photos, your eye is drawn straight to the color. The photo could include one hundred children, but only the child in color catches your attention. The rest of the picture blends into the background.

Life-giving leaders are the splash of color in a monochrome organiza-tion. Your attention goes to them. Your focus finds the leaders who are bringing life to the team. You notice life-giving leaders because they go out of their way to share an encouraging word or celebrate a great decision made by someone on the staff. When leaders get intentional about bringing life into the organization, it's amazing the way it makes other leaders feel.

Have you ever heard someone say, "When I was with (fill in the

blank), I felt as if I was with Jesus"? Basically they are saying the person rubbed off on them. They were lifted up by the other person's spiritual countenance and wisdom. Life-giving leaders rub off on you. When you're with one, you will know it. It will be as if they leave you better than when you started.

WHO CARES?

All this talk about beauty and art and splashes of color . . . What does that have to do with leadership?

Everything.

Life can grow and flourish only in environments where the nutrients and conditions are right. There's a reason the Dead Sea is called the Dead Sea. Because of the sea's extreme salinity, life can't flourish there. On the other hand, if you ever visit a rain forest or a tropical island, you will see abundance. Life to the fullest. Flowers, fruit trees, grasses, and wildlife have everything they need to grow and have life.

It is no different for organizations. People will not stay in places where growth and abundance are absent. We have a divine directive, remember? We are called to create spaces in which life can explode, where leaders can flourish.

- What are you doing in staff meetings to grow and help your team take deep root?
- Does your organization have toxic problems? What are you doing to address them?
- What areas in your business are gray right now and need color? What is your next step to bring life to one of the areas?
- Which leaders around you grab your attention because they bring color? How can you encourage them to do even more along those lines?
- How are you enhancing the culture?

To create amazing cultures we have to consider what we allow to in-filtrate and make the culture unhealthy. Where do you need to add abundance and color in your organization? Are there leaders, teams, or divisions that don't let life flourish? Take an inventory of the areas that need work. You have to do this.

I learned years ago that leadership isn't just what you do but what you allow. Where are you allowing leaders to operate counter to the culture you are trying to create? Leaders at any level of the org chart need to be able to identify the areas and people who are toxic to the plan, who create gray and monochrome environments, who keep others from thriving. You have to pinpoint the issues and make changes. Now.

15

From Seed to Fruit

Life-Giving Leaders Build
Teams That Flourish

I love teams. I've *loved being* on teams since I was younger than five years old.

I was a part of the Bandits. We wore red-and-black jerseys that had a sweet logo of a bandit on the left chest. The best part (and the part that was brand-new to me) was that eight other people were wearing the same uniform. We looked like a million bucks. Second only to looking good, the goal was to learn how to play together as a team. Again, a brand-new concept for me.

I loved it. Passing, dribbling, talking to one another, and, of course, winning. Together. There is something about winning with other people that can never be replicated on your own. Wrestling is an individual sport in which the team earns points only when a team member is awarded points. Similar to golf, tennis, cross-country, and track-and-field, individual sports are still more fun to me when they are done as a team.

What I'm saying is that nothing else in the world can replicate the experience of being on a great team. A life-giving team might very well be one of the greatest gifts we can give to leaders. I would bet that many of us would choose to make less money if we got to be on a team that we loved and felt connected to.

Thousands of books have been written about what makes a great team. Honestly, other than self-leadership, I can't think of a subject I enjoy researching and working on more. High-capacity, life-giving teams change the game. When teams win championships, people are on top of the world. When they don't, it's tough to stay motivated. Teams can be amazing or they can be brutal. They can be life-giving or they can suck the life out of you. When you have to complete a task that requires you to rely on your team, it doesn't take long to figure out the condition of the team you're on.

I could easily talk through hundreds of attributes of great teams or walk through examples of amazing teams in history and what made them great. The Dream Team, Green Bay Packers, Chicago Bulls, or any Atlanta sports team. (Okay, that last one's a joke, but after forty-plus years of cheering, I still believe!) These teams can serve as an awesome model of great teamwork.[1]

When you become a life-giving leader, you gain the ability to develop life-giving teams. The entire goal of becoming a life-giving leader is to allow life to flow from you to others. This is where the rubber hits the road. If there's one group that should be affected most by your leadership, it's your team. Maybe your team is just you and your family. Maybe it's a department of one hundred people. Either way, your leadership will have impact. It is mission-critical for a successful organization to have life-giving teams. In many instances, leaders think they must have a great team because they've created a great product. It's not usually the case. Often the teams aren't being built; they are being used. You will get more out of your leaders when they are more than a means to an end, more than just numbers on a list. They need to be seen as leaders and teams that can contribute with ideas and leadership. This matters because *how* you operate as a team is just as important as what you accomplish.

COUNTERFEIT WIN

This is another topic that could fill a book in and of itself. The first time I heard about the counterfeit win, I thought it might be one of the most powerful leadership concepts I'd ever heard. I was right. This is mission-critical for teams that don't want to stop with success; they want to flourish.

Here's the principle: *a good product with a bad process is a counterfeit win.*

That's it. It's short and to the point, and I wouldn't be surprised if you just had a punched-in-the-gut moment.

You might be experiencing counterfeit wins every time you go to work. You will feel it when you are part of this type of success. At the moment the results come in or the project is completed or the contract is signed or a new client raves about your team's work, it feels like a win. But when you think back to the process involved in getting there, you know inside it was pretty terrible. The means to accomplish the end wasn't something you'd want to tell a friend about.

Let's say you're on a church staff. You're having great success with new visitors. The Sunday services seem off-the-charts good. The church is growing in many areas, more kids show up than you have space for, young adults want to be involved and serve, and giving has reached higher levels than ever before. All things are a go.

Except for one little problem.

The team is unhealthy. Everyone needs to take Mondays off. Not to recover from being tired, but because no one wants to be in the same room with each other on Monday. The stress over the weekend was so high that on Mondays staff members are ready to hide in a dark room. The team culture is toxic. Areas are in silos, isolated, because there is no connection or healthy relationships. Teams work together only because they have to, not because they want to.

Meanwhile, the target market loves what your team is doing. On weekends they experience your "product," and the next weekend they come back for more. It's the best they have seen. Given the response to what you're doing, how could you not be winning? The audience is growing, and anyone serving on any church staff would count this as a huge success, right?

But to you it feels as if you're losing. That's why it's counterfeit. It feels like one thing to those outside your organization or team and something totally different to those involved behind the scenes, to those who are *in* the process. When there is a deep discrepancy between experience for some and reality for others, the counterfeit win is fully alive. And it's not just that you and other staff members can see behind the curtain. It's because counterfeit wins are not sustainable. Staff members will leave, and new staff will arrive and then leave. The ones who stay will burn out and lose their effectiveness. Some of them will become even more toxic and will poison what remains.

Some or all of this is likely to take place, and then the whole thing will hit a tipping point—a point of no return, the place where the wins cease. You've probably either seen this from a distance or you've experienced it yourself.

Leaders fight for a healthy process. As a matter of fact, they will settle for nothing less. They want not only an amazing product but also the ability to enjoy creating it with their team!

I don't know any business leader who likes high turnover. Unless it's a leader who turns over staff like crazy as he or she keeps looking for people who can just get it done, no matter the cost.

I'm talking about that. I'm referring to a team that is committed to the mission but is disturbed by the way the mission is accomplished. This is the opposite of life-giving leadership. Life-giving leaders have life-giving teams, and they retain staff much longer than their counterparts. One of the most frequent questions asked by leaders in business, ministry, and the nonprofit world alike is this: How do you find and keep good talent? The answer is simple: Make your workplace life-giving. Make it irresistible. You have the title. You get to create the culture.

Leaders, we can't settle for counterfeit wins. Often when we make short-term decisions instead of investing in long-term play, such as culture and team building, we end up losing. It might provide a quick and easy win, but it will not benefit you in the long run.

It feels good to get that off my chest. Now let's look at three ways to avoid counterfeit wins and create life-giving teams.

Trust Versus Suspicion

I had the chance to learn from one of the best leadership thinkers on the planet: Andy Stanley. I know this is probably the hundredth time I've quoted him in this book, but I've seen that what he teaches works. I have held on to one of his concepts about getting new staff members started off right. Right when they join the team, they are exposed to this concept. Here it is:

> When there's a gap in information, you have a choice. You can choose to trust the person or you can choose to be suspicious. Great teams choose to trust each other when there is a gap in information.

Let's say a member of the team is late to a meeting. Everyone else is there. Except this one person. (People showing up late to meetings is my pet peeve, so it makes sense for this to be my example.) No one has heard from the person who is missing. Now everyone in the room has a choice to make.

Choosing suspicion would sound like

- "Ugh. He's always late."
- "She doesn't care about the rest of us. All she cares about is herself."
- "He's the boss's favorite, so he can do whatever he wants."
- "She probably overslept because she was out all night doing who knows what."

Choosing trust would sound like

- "She must have a great reason. It's not like her to be late."
- "I wonder if he was informed of the meeting time."
- "He usually communicates well, so I'll check in to make sure everything is okay."

You might be thinking that choosing trust is too neutral. What if the person is late *all the time*? If that's the case, then a different conversation is needed. In that instance, I don't have to choose trust over suspicion. The person's history fills in the information gap, and I proceed based on the person's history.

When something comes up that could cause conflict, I tell my team, "Fill the gap with facts, and then we don't have to make a choice." However, if we, as a team, have to make a choice, we choose to believe the best. We choose trust.

If you want to be an amazing team member, build a ton of trust by filling all your gaps with good information. Then choose to trust the people around you. Believe in them.

Life-giving teams are built on this type of foundation.

ADVOCATE FOR ONE ANOTHER

Trust versus suspicion and being one another's advocates go hand in hand. They build on each other. Once you've established a foundation of trust, then you can choose to fight for one another. Life-giving leaders understand that they *must* champion the people God has entrusted to them.

Great team members will stand up for their teammates, no matter what. There's a reason benches clear during a baseball game when a teammate gets beaned at the plate. It's a show of strength and unity. There's a reason some teams walk onto the field arm in arm. They are showing the other side they have one another's backs.

I was introduced to this idea when I was in third grade. We were playing two-on-two football. You either run the ball yourself or hand it off. Not much strategy. One of the kids in the neighborhood liked to pick on people. He was about a year older than me, and he was a pretty decent athlete. On this day, skinny Tyler was ready to hold his ground.

The neighborhood bully and my brother were on a team together, and the bully ran the ball on every play. He thought he was God's gift to all sports. Finally, my brother called him out on it and all of a sudden it got ugly. The bully pushed my brother, and then he took a swing at him.

You might recall what I said earlier about my boyhood size and strength. In third grade I wasn't the picture of masculinity. The wind could blow and change my direction.

On that day it didn't matter. I'd had enough. I wasn't going to stand by and let my older brother get pushed around. Have you ever seen the 1983 movie *A Christmas Story,* the scene where Ralphie Parker loses it on Scott Farkas? Well, that was yours truly. I lost it.

I jumped on the neighborhood bully and took him down. (Let me point out that I don't preach that fighting is okay. I'm just telling you a story about being tough for once in my life.) I think this incident lasted fewer seconds than my first wrestling match, but I came out on top in this one. I suspect the sheer sight of my coming after him was the last thing the bully expected. Me too. He took off after I landed one punch and ran all the way to his house while I chased him as if my pants were on fire.

For a hot minute, I was beyond proud. Then reality set in. My parents would be home soon, and there was zero chance I wouldn't get in trouble for this one. Which I did. I received a stern talking-to about fighting and how it isn't worth it and whatnot. Secretly, I wasn't thinking about the punishment. I was still pumped I had won the fight.

Here's why I tell this story. Although it was wrong to fight, it wasn't wrong to be an advocate for my brother. He's family. We're on the same team. I stood up for him.

When you choose to be an advocate for one of your teammates, he or she will never forget it and it will change your relationship. It draws you together. And guess what? That person will now be *your* advocate. Crazy, I know, but it's true. So choose to support your teammates. Believe in them. Bring life to them and show them you are their advocate. It could be as simple as listening to your teammates during meetings to help support their idea. Sometimes it means confronting a peer because you want to be their advocate in helping them grow professionally. It could be that you've heard people talking about a teammate and you need to set the record straight.

Think of a time when someone stood up for you at work. Maybe it was a peer. Maybe it was your boss. Either way, didn't it make you want to do the same for that person? This is crazy powerful. Team members who choose to be advocates for one another will change the game.

View One Another's Gifts as Keys to Success

Not to beat a dead horse, but these principles build on one another. When you are fighting against counterfeit wins, you choose to build your team on a foundation of trust. Often that trust is built by advocating for one another. You will be amazed at how quickly team members can achieve greater performance and health when they stand up for one another.

After building a team like that, this last principle will be easy. Everything in this book has been written so you can see how important this last point is.

Each Person Has Something Unique to Offer Your Team

It's not exclusively the team leader's job to know the uniqueness of each team member. It's also the team's job. If you're on a lacrosse team, it might be the coach's job to figure out the best formation or plays in light of the team's skills, but it is also the job of the players. The team needs to be aware of its unique skills so the players can use them at the right time. If you know one of your offensive players has a secret burst of speed, use it strategically. Players need to know that as well as the coach.

Life-giving leaders become the best students of their team members' unique contributions. In business, we need to know that our financial team is making us financially intelligent and they are keeping us above reproach. When you trust that's happening, it allows the operations team to fire on all cylinders, not having to look over their shoulders and wonder if the finances are in order.

At the office, it's not enough for the boss to strategically position each person to best utilize his or her unique attributes. It requires everyone. (Peer accountability is much more powerful than relying only on the boss to hold employees accountable.)

Even NBA legend LeBron James needs good players around him to win games. Superstars don't exist without help. They couldn't do what they do without a team in place, working hard to get the job done. While it's rare that any organization has the Michael Jordan of accounting or the Joe Montana of sales, organizations can work hard at building and using their teams to accomplish great things. It happens only when the team is firing on all cylinders and the leaders are working in synergy.

I know this is a crazy thought, but it's good business to trust people. Obviously, there's a chance someone will prove to be untrustworthy. But just because you had a bad cup of coffee once doesn't mean you stop drinking coffee. Just because someone once used you and lost your trust doesn't mean everyone who works with you should be called into suspicion. By the way, when people are operating as life-giving leaders through their unique God wiring, you will find they are worthy of trust. They are at their best and you will reap the benefits of their abilities for the mission.

Life-giving leaders, until you focus on intentionally building a great team, you will miss out on one of the greatest joys of leadership. Team building and orchestrating a group of unique leaders is leadership legacy at its finest.

How About You?

Achieving amazing things with amazing teams is a leadership legacy that's worthy of pursuit.

Life-giving leaders bring color to monochrome organizations and they build amazing teams. The truth is, there is one additional component that will take leaders to the next level. It's what separates leaders who will build lasting influence from those who might gain temporary, fleeting influence.

How are your teams? Are you able to change the culture of your organization by bringing color to your area of responsibility? If counterfeit wins are becoming evident, what can you do to rectify the situation? Are you a trustworthy teammate and pulling your weight to create an outstanding team? What's missing from making your current team high-capacity and life-giving?

16

O Captain! My Captain!

Life-Giving Leaders Leave a Legacy

love technology and working with my hands. In high school I took technology classes. I loved the subject, but I loved the teacher even more.

Coach Vander Velde became a mentor to me. He taught with such grace and love. His faith was on display every day in the way he served his students. He was a life-giving leader. He poured life into all of us, and a few of us were blessed to have him as a mentor. We worked together to build his house, and he taught me skills and life lessons along the way. He led from a place of fully accepting who he was and what God had gifted him to do. It was amazing to watch.

Even in a public school setting where teachers and staff find they need to be strategic about expressing their faith, he was comfortable and confident in himself. Not many leaders have had a more profound impact on who I am than Coach Vander Velde.

Here is another example from one of my favorite movies. Okay, I enjoy movies and sports. I'm convinced that nine out of the top ten narratives that have been most helpful to me over the years have been related to either sports or movies. So if you haven't seen *Dead Poets Society*, stop reading this book and go watch it now.

In the movie, a life-giving leader changes lives. Robin Williams's portrayal of English teacher John Keating moved millions of viewers. The story is set at Welton Academy, a Vermont boarding school for boys. Most of the boys are shipped off to Welton each year, where they live away from home and contend with unrealistic expectations and difficult scenarios. Most of their teachers are the opposite of life-giving, lacking energy and excitement.

Keating had been a student at Welton, and in the movie he has returned to teach English. He is the youngest faculty member and most likely the most progressive. But what matters is that Keating changes the lives of his students by being a life-giving leader. He is inspiring, confident, and funny. He is real, authentic, and aware. He pushes and pulls his students to think differently. He serves them like crazy and cares for them. He brings life to a dead environment.

The most well-known scene in the movie shows this happening. In one of Keating's first interactions with the boys, he inspires the students to seize the day (*carpe diem*) and see the world from a new perspective. He teaches them Walt Whitman's famous poem "O Captain! My Captain!" written about the incredible leader Abraham Lincoln. Through literature and poetry, Keating inspires his students to live original lives and be who they were made to be. He urges them to figure out who they are. He uses poetry, literature, and communication to inspire them to live *their* lives, not lives prescribed to them by anyone else. He empowers his students to think for themselves and be themselves.

Have you ever been around leaders who had such an impact on your life that you would do anything for them? That's what Keating does for the boys at Welton. He eventually pushes them so far in their exploration and inspiration that he winds up getting fired. The climactic scene takes place the day Keating comes to retrieve his things. The boys are listening to a boring lecture from a substitute teacher. As Keating is leaving, the boys stand up and shout, "O Captain! My Captain!"[1]

Life flowed from John Keating. He was a life-giving leader who embodied everything we've talked about. The boys were better men because of his leadership. He pulled their uniqueness out of them and changed them forever.

This might be over the top for some of you, but I think it's true. When you are led by someone who brings you life and encourages you to lean into your uniqueness, it changes you. It will affect you for the rest of your life.

You can't be life-giving to others if you have nothing to give, but you can change lives when you have life to give. I can't express how amazing it is to spend time around men and women who lead from their uniqueness. This process we've been talking about made them into the leaders they are today.

If you as a leader work to embrace this process, you will forever be changed and you will forever change the leaders around you. This isn't easy. Many leaders will accomplish some of these steps but not all of them. On the other hand, I have seen many leaders climb to the top. They lead from a comfortable place because they lead from their truest selves. The end of this identity search is the beginning of a new leadership season. It changes you and the people around you, but it won't happen overnight.

Again, things of value require sacrifice. Leadership is no exception. Becoming aware of yourself requires heavy lifting, but authenticity is worth the discomfort it requires. The deep, inward work of self-acceptance will free you to be life-giving. The powerful posture of confidence without arrogance will be a lifelong dance. Your pursuit of humility will attract others, and it's worth it. *You* are worth it, and the leaders you lead are worth the work.

Think about a couple of leaders who have had that type of impact on you. People who spoke life into you through the way they served you. They poured life into you. They modeled life-giving leadership.

LIFE-GIVING LEADERS IN ACTION

A number of people have poured life into me. They brought color to the gray areas of my life. They served as a catalyst for my faith and leadership journey. I'll share a couple of examples that span multiple spaces of my life. These leaders, who represent different spheres of influence, changed my life forever.

My Wife

As I have mentioned previously, Carrie has been one of the most life-giving people in my life. She's an example of how to love people well. She's one of the most loyal and life-giving friends to her friends and to me. She can see through the junk and pull out the beauty. I'm a better leader because Carrie is standing with me. Our ministry together is way more effective because we partner together. I don't have enough words to adequately thank her and explain how life-giving she is to me and our boys.

My Family

My dad and granddad have influenced my leadership in similar ways but also in different ways. My dad taught me more about being myself than anyone else. He's an amazing example of a person who embraces his uniqueness. He tries to bring joy to everyone he meets. He showed me how to care for people and how to love my wife unconditionally. He has taught me more than he realizes about being my authentic self. He modeled it for me without having to use words. My mom and my dad showed up. They loved each other unconditionally, and they loved my brother and me in the same way.

Poppy, my granddad, was another early and powerful role model. He was larger than life. A fire chief in Atlanta, he carried himself with poise and self-respect. He protected and cared for my grandmother in an extraordinary fashion. Both he and my dad worked harder than anyone I've ever known. I learned what it means to be humble from my granddad. He was a big deal, but he would never let on to that. When we ran into his old colleagues or friends, I could see the impact he had made on them. He was an awesome man.

He was an example of the type of life-giving leader who poured out his life for those around him. His family, friends, and colleagues benefited as he served them. He was joyful and lived a vibrant life. Doesn't that sound like someone you want to be around?

Pastors

Earlier I mentioned Tom Tanner, the Wesley Foundation director at the University of Georgia. God put Tom in my life at the right time to change me forever. My spiritual growth skyrocketed during my few years there. My leadership grew as I started to understand how to lead people spiritually. I watched an amazing man devote hours to praying for us.

There was a small group of guys who would gather at midnight on Sunday nights at Tom's house to pray. He poured his life into ours. He loved his wife and kids well. He preached the roof off the building. More than any of that, he led us students into a deeper walk with our Lord. What's amazing to me is that Tom started his season there wondering if God had put him in the right place. When I was a part of the ministry, you would never have believed he had asked those questions early on. He had such confidence in his calling that it inspired me. He pushed me to be a better leader in my relationships and in my work.

How has someone's confidence in calling influenced your life?

You Never Know . . .

You never know who will make a lasting impact on your life. It might be a leader you are close to for years or it could be someone you're around for only a few days or a moment.

My youth pastor in high school had an abundant-life mentality. I can also point to many of my soccer coaches, professors, and pastors. Robert Coleman, who wrote the book *The Master Plan of Evangelism,* discipled me in seminary. Archbishop Foley Beach was my pastor when I was youth pastor at St. Alban's Episcopal Church.

Over the past ten years, I have worked alongside some of the greatest church leaders of our generation. Andy Stanley leads with the highest integrity and love for people. Craig Groeschel has invested in me as a communicator and leader.

In my forty-plus years on earth, God has poured His life into me through amazing men and women. My teams at Browns Bridge and Catalyst have poured more life into me than I can say.

My wife and my boys are the most amazing givers of life I could ask for. I have wonderful friends.

I'm telling you this for one purpose. Wouldn't you want people to thank you one day because you poured life into them? I'm praying that I will have that impact on someone, and I'm praying you will have that impact on others.

The other side of leadership is also a fact. I could make a list of men and women who have taken life from me. People who have taught me how not to lead. People who caused me to lose trust in leaders. People who hurt my faith. They are the antithesis of life-giving leaders. Unfortunately, that list may be longer than the list of those who made me better. A day cannot go by in which we stop seeking life-giving leadership.

You have the option to choose which list you land on. The hard work is worth every minute of it.

O Captain! My Captain!   179

When Life Flows, Influence Grows

I recently went on a trip with some amazing Christian men. Every night we had dinner and shared our stories. One of the men in the group is a living legend. He has been behind many of the culture-shaping ministries you're familiar with. He knows more people than you can imagine.

He is a leader in his seventies who gave us everything he had. He said he wanted to make sure to leave nothing in the tank when his time on earth is through. The response in the room was beautiful. The high-capacity and influential leaders in the room hung on every word he said. The men who didn't know this man could tell he was worthy of respect and honor. Those of us who knew him honored him with our words and prayers.

I couldn't help but think, *This is what a life-giving leader looks like. This is someone whose river of influence has brought fruit and life to so many, and his beautiful legacy shows it.*

That's how I want to end this race: grateful and surrounded by leaders whom God has allowed me to influence in a life-giving way. I pray that's your desire too. To have a river of influence that creates lasting beauty and life for everything that gets near it. I have a feeling you are aiming for that. You are created with the beauty of the Lord within you. He made you unique for a unique purpose. You can bring life to those around you in ways most of us can't imagine. The quicker you embrace and lead from your truest self, the quicker you will see God's calling fulfilled in your life and leadership.

Leaders, the pursuit of life-giving leadership begins and ends with Jesus. As I have mentioned, my faith is central to my leadership. It has directed me for the past twenty-five years and will continue to do so. Jesus is the clearest and most complete picture of how leaders should lead. Leadership should center on bringing life to others. Jesus brings life to people. It only makes sense that they go hand in hand.

If you have read thus far, thank you.

My charge to you is to go and lead as if people's lives depend on your leadership, because they do. Pour life into others to build a life-giving leadership legacy. There is no greater pursuit for our leadership. Seek first the kingdom and lead from that posture. God will serve alongside you, and it will be the most fulfilling adventure of your life. People are worth our best. Go and be a life-giving leader!

Acknowledgments

I want to say thank you to a million people. My story and belief system have been built by the leaders God has put directly in my life and by those I've never met but who have influenced me with their books and ministries. Leadership is contagious—good and bad. I'm thankful to the men and women whose shoulders I'm standing on who have helped shape my faith and leadership.

Thank you to my wife and boys for being the most life-giving leaders in my world. You three are why I do what I do. I believe we are in this together to serve the church for the rest of our lives, and I'm grateful for the opportunity to learn from you. I love you fiercely.

Thank you to my mom, dad, and Jason. You guys made life fun and had an impact on my leadership. I'll meet you at Ryan's or Golden Corral! Love you.

Thank you to Ray, Peggy, and all of the Boohers for loving and supporting me.

Thank you to my team at Catalyst. I have never truly understood why God would gift you to me to lead. To Chrissi, Daniel, LVZ, the management team, and the staff. I don't deserve a team with such passion, love, and fire for leaders who love the church. You inspire me to be life giving by how you love the leaders we serve. You are Catalyst embodied. Thank you.

Thank you to my Browns Bridge SPD team who helped me define my leadership in the early days and who helped me fight through all the principles in this book. You gave me grace when I needed it. Hopefully you became better leaders as a result of our time together.

Thank you to all the leaders who've hired me, invested in me, evaluated me, and spoken life into me. Andy Stanley, Craig Groeschel, Lane Jones, Bob Goff, Robert Coleman, Archbishop (with great hats) Foley Beach, Julie Arnold, Fran LaMattina, Clay Scroggins, Todd Vander Velde, Brad Lomenick, Dionne van Zyl, Franklin Scott, and countless others.

A huge shout-out to Tom Tanner and all our Wesley crew. Who knew that twenty-plus years ago God was growing a tiny community that would make such an impact in the world? God did. Maybe that's what the whole "dark globe with lights on it" meant that Melissa kept telling us about!

To some of my best friends in the world who have stood with me for decades. Thank you for being life for me when I needed it and occasionally laughing at my jokes! Steve Hambrick, Ashley Hill, Elliott Moon, Ryan Shove, Chris Priestaf, Kane Lester, and Brain (that's right . . . Brain!) Cole: You guys have been some of the greatest friends any man could ask for. I don't have enough words to say thank you.

A big thank-you to some of the key leaders who helped me make this project happen! Ana Munoz (my amazing assistant and proofreader extraordinaire), Erin Blonshine (for reading this way too early on), Lindsay van Zyl (for caring as much about getting the word out for this as I do), and Corinne Kutz (for designing this incredible cover)—your friendship and hard work on this book will never be forgotten. You are each legends in my eyes, and your work will influence leaders all over!

Thank you to my editor—and now friend—Andrew Stoddard for helping make this a book I'm proud of. Thank you to the Yates & Yates crew for representing me so well throughout this process. Thank you, WaterBrook, for the chance to publish this project. It has been a gift to me.

Thank you to all the believers that are fighting day in and day out to lead well and make the biggest kingdom impact possible. I'm honored to serve alongside you as we lift the name of Jesus together.

Notes

Chapter 1: It's Just Your Personality

1. Ty Kiisel, "65% of Americans Choose a Better Boss over a Raise—Here's Why," *Forbes,* October 16, 2012, www.forbes.com /sites/tykiisel/2012/10/16/65-of-americans-choose-a-better-boss -over-a-raise-heres-why/#4810270276d2.

Chapter 2: Divine Directive

1. Joe McAlpine, "#OC16: Save a Life, Andy Stanley," Slingshot Group, April 28, 2016, http://slingshotgroup.org/oc16-save-life -andy-stanley.

Chapter 3: No Regrets

1. Bronnie Ware, "Regrets of the Dying," Bronnieware.com, www .bronnieware.com/blog/regrets-of-the-dying.
2. For a tremendous treatment of this and the other love languages, see Gary Chapman, *The Five Love Languages: The Secret to Love That Lasts* (Chicago: Northfield, 2015).

Chapter 4: Made Especially for Leadership

1. For more on this type of courage, see Joshua 1:9.
2. "Made in His Image: The Amazing Design of the Human Body," *Acts & Facts* 44, no. 10 (2015), www.icr.org/article/made-his -image-amazing-design-human; Susan DeRemer, "20 Facts About the Amazing Eye," Discovery Eye Foundation, June 10, 2014, http://discoveryeye.org/20-facts-about-the-amazing-eye.

Part 2: Releasing the Life Giver Within You

1. *Merriam-Webster,* s.v. "authentic," www.merriam-webster.com
   /dictionary/authentic.
2. Brené Brown, *The Gifts of Imperfection: Let Go of Who You
   Think You're Supposed to Be and Embrace Who You Are*
   (Center City, MN: Hazelden, 2010), 49.

Chapter 6: Schoolyard Sports

1. *Talladega Nights: The Ballad of Ricky Bobby,* directed by
   Adam McKay (Culver City, CA: Columbia Pictures, 2006);
   "Talladega Nights: The Ballad of Ricky Bobby: Quotes,"
   IMDb, www.imdb.com/title/tt0415306/quotes?ref_=tt_ql
   _trv_4.
2. "Tom Brady Talks to Steve Kroft," *60 Minutes,* November
   4, 2005, www.cbsnews.com/news/transcript-tom-brady
   -part-3.
3. "Tom Brady Talks to Steve Kroft."

Chapter 7: It's Like Riding a Bike

1. Vince Lombardi Jr., comp., *The Essential Vince Lombardi:
   Words and Wisdom to Motivate, Inspire, and Win* (New York:
   McGraw-Hill, 2003), 41.

Chapter 8: Something Bigger

1. Rick Warren, *The Purpose Driven Life: What on Earth Am I
   Here For?* (Grand Rapids, MI: Zondervan, 2012), 190–91.
2. Encyclopedia.com, s.v. "attitude," www.encyclopedia.com
   /social-sciences-and-law/political-science-and-government
   /military-affairs-nonnaval/attitude.

Chapter 9: At the Top of Your Game

1. Keith Urban, "Gone Tomorrow (Here Today)," by Keith Urban, Jeff Bhasker, and Samuel Tyler Johnson, *Ripcord*, copyright © 2016, Hit Red Records.
2. Sam Chand (Catalyst staff meeting, Suwanee, GA, April 28, 2015).

Chapter 10: A Call to Sweat

1. Simon Sinek, Session 8 (speech, Catalyst Atlanta, Atlanta, GA, October 7, 2016).
2. Martin Luther King Jr., "What Is Your Life's Blueprint?" (speech, Barratt Junior High School, Philadelphia, PA, October 26, 1967).
3. Peter Economy, "Mark Cuban: 19 Inspiring Power Quotes for Success," *Inc.*, March 20, 2015, www.inc.com/peter-economy/mark-cuban-19-inspiring-power-quotes-for-success.html.

Chapter 11: A Call to Sacrifice

1. Simon Sinek, Session 8 (speech, Catalyst Atlanta, Atlanta, GA, October 7, 2016).
2. Andy Stanley (speech, Catalyst One Day, Austin, TX, August 21, 2014).
3. George J. Flynn, foreword to *Leaders Eat Last: Why Some Teams Pull Together and Others Don't*, Simon Sinek (New York: Penguin, 2017), xii.
4. Max Lucado, *When God Whispers Your Name: Discover the Path to Hope in Knowing That God Cares for You* (Nashville, TN: Thomas Nelson, 1999), 44.

5. John C. Maxwell, *Winning with People: Discover the People Principles That Work for You Every Time* (Nashville, TN: Thomas Nelson, 2004), 91.

Chapter 12: A Call to Surrender

1. Andy Stanley, *When Work and Family Collide: Keeping Your Job from Cheating Your Family* (Colorado Springs, CO: Multnomah, 2011).
2. Jim Collins, "Looking Out for Number One," Jim Collins, June 1996, www.jimcollins.com/article_topics/articles/looking-out.html.
3. Graham Cooke, telephone conversation with the author and Dionne van Zyl, April 25, 2017.

Chapter 13: A Call to Serve

1. *Hacksaw Ridge,* directed by Mel Gibson (Santa Monica, CA: Summit Entertainment, 2016).
2. "*Hacksaw Ridge:* Quotes," IMDb, www.imdb.com/title/tt211 9532/quotes?ref_=tt_ql_trv_4.
3. Eliza Berman, "The True Story Behind *Hacksaw Ridge,*" *Time,* November 3, 2016, http://time.com/4539373/hacksaw-ridge -movie-true-story.

Chapter 14: The Wizard of Oz

1. *The Wizard of Oz,* directed by Victor Fleming et al (Beverly Hills, CA: Metro-Goldwyn-Mayer, 1939).
2. Patrick Lencioni, *The Advantage: Why Organizational Health Trumps Everything Else in Business* (San Francisco: Jossey-Bass, 2012), 5, italics in original.
3. The phrase comes from Andy Stanley.
4. *Oxford Living Dictionaries,* s.v. "worth," https://en.oxford dictionaries.com/definition/us/worth.

Chapter 15: From Seed to Fruit

1. In regard to teams, my all-time favorite book is Patrick Lencioni's *The Five Dysfunctions of a Team: A Leadership Fable* (San Francisco: Jossey-Bass, 2002). It's the best.

Chapter 16: O Captain! My Captain!

1. *Dead Poets Society,* directed by Peter Weir (Burbank, CA: Touchstone Pictures, 1989).

FOLLOW

TYLER REAGIN

TR° **TYLERREAGIN.COM**

Find Tyler on social
@TYLERREAGIN

For all speaking inquiries please
visit tylerreagin.com